Get cooking
chicos
muchos besos y
abrazos

Jacqui

Finn

Fergal

Angus
xx

ALL
TAPAS
110 recipes

ESCUDO DE ORO

ALL TAPAS
© for the texts: Remedios Vázquez Fdez. de Liencres and Ángel de Miguel
© for the photographs: SIMPEI, S.L. and IBERIMAGE (pages 4, 5, 6, 7, 8 and 9)
© for the present edition in this and any other language:
EDITORIAL FISA ESCUDO DE ORO, S.A.

Layout and printing entirely designed and
produced by the technical teams at
EDITORIAL FISA ESCUDO DE ORO S.A.

Copyright for the present edition as regards
photographs and literary text:
© EDITORIAL FISA ESCUDO DE ORO, S.A.
www.eoro.com

ISBN: 978-84-378-2692-9
Legal Deposit: 29389-2008
Printed in Spain

THE WONDERFUL WORLD OF TAPAS

Tapas have conquered the world. This form of dining, eating snacks whilst standing, really more a form of social relations, has its origins in taverns and bars in Andalusia where, once upon a time, a slice of cold meat, cheese or even bread was used to cover ("tapar" in Spanish) to prevent flies and mosquitoes from entering the precious drink or, according to other versions, to stop this generous wine from losing any of its exquisite aroma. Later, by now known as tapas, the system evolved into what many refer to as "the art of eating on one's feet".

Although Andalusia is, without doubt, the cradle and home of the tapa, the practice is now widespread all over Spain, and perhaps more popular in the Basque Country than any other region, for here bar counters display huge ranges of "pintxos", creative masterpieces combining design and exquisite combinations of flavours. Nowadays, families and groups of friends frequently decide to have a "tapa dinner", often choosing to stand at the bar to rather than the more comfortable option of a table and chairs.

There are many different types of tapa in Spain; there are traditional tapas found in all regions (who would dare to say that the potato omelette comes originally from this or that place?); those typical of each differ-

ent area, region or autonomous community; so-called "designer tapas", the fruit of their creators' imagination (some more successful than others, if the truth be known); and what we might call "imported" tapas, new arrivals gradually taking up their place in this variegated world of tapas. Not forgetting, of course, what we might call "pure" ingredients: for example, cheese, cold cuts, shellfish and dried fruit.

And what do we drink with tapas? The answer is, whatever we fancy, in whatever order we prefer. Even soft drinks of all kind, though, in our opinion, this option is not recommended, except in the case of children

or people who cannot tolerate alcohol, even in minimal amounts. In such cases, the best solution is a glass of cool, clear water.

Beer is amongst the drinks most frequently chosen to accompany tapas. Spain boasts dozens of brands and varieties of this popular beverage, most of them unanimously judged excellent in quality by locals and visitors alike. Though beer can be found everywhere in bottles and cans, the most typical way of drinking it is in the form of a draught "caña", a small glass served up from the barrel. Beer is an excellent accompaniment for practically all tapas, particularly those containing vinegar.

Turning now to wine, this is nearly always served in bottles, though it used to be served up from the barrel, a practice becoming more and more unusual these days. Wine by the glass, whether red, white or rosé, tends to be from the region where it is consumed, and its quality, though high, rarely matches that of the more prestigious brands which, except in certain establishments which serve these superior wines by the glass, can only be consumed by the bottle. This will generally not present a problem for those dining in groups, as a bottle, well-served, contains around seven glasses.

Fortified or liqueur wines, known in Spain as *vinos generosos*, are a different case. Such wines are usually served by the glass – the classical *catavinos* tasting glass – though it is also easy to find half bottles (37.5 cl) in Spain, especially in Andalusia. This is an excellent measure for two people, particularly in the case of fino and manzanilla wines, as the more powerful varieties, such as *oloroso seco* and amontillado, should be consumed in moderation, particularly if one is not used to them, as over consumption can produce undesired results.

Another classical beverage in Spain is vermouth, known here as "vermú". Less popular these days, this drink still has many fans and though found mostly in bottle, real enthusiasts tend to prefer it from the barrel, served from a tap. Even rare variants on vermouth can also be found, such as the typical *palo* in Majorca.

And although, as we have mentioned, many other possibilities exist, such as certain cocktails (a Dry Martini, for example), these are much more rarely found. Re-

ally, the only drink we have not yet listed here is sparkling wine, or cava. Most cava is produced in Catalonia, although it is also made in other Spanish regions, such as La Rioja, Extremadura and Aragon. The advantage of this exceptional beverage is that it is a perfect accompaniment for any dish. Cava is ideal for the warmer months, the varieties "brut" and "brut nature" best for tapas. It should be served chilled to between 6 and 8° C, whilst wider glasses are becoming more popular of late for drinking sparkling wine from, displacing the classical fluted "flauta". It all depends on one's taste.

Now, then, having completed this summary of the delicious beverages that will accompany us on our journey through the world of tapas, we can go on to consider the most authentic places where tapas are served, and the most attractive specialities in each region.

Firstly, Andalusia, the cradle of the tapa in almost all its variants, as we have mentioned previously. Although tapas, often served free to accompany drinks, can generally be ordered from a long menu or list offered to customers, another practice is also to consume portions or half portions ("raciones" or "medias raciones"), which are larger than tapas and perfect for sharing. There are a practically infinite number of restaurants, bars, taverns and other establishments, such as the typical *ventas*, serving tapas in this region, whilst prices are generally reasonable. Though many prefer to stand at the bar, greater comfort in the form of a table is usually also available. Though fino is

shellfish, fried and in batter, along with small pots of seafood dishes. Inland, we can try different types of meat tapas (*mechada, albondiguillas, flamenquines*) whilst, elsewhere, we should not miss the superb Andalusian cold cuts, popular in Huelva, Granada and other areas.

A good selection of fish and shellfish tapas is also available along the Mediterranean coastline, served in bars and terraces or pavement cafés, accompanied by good beer or excellent wine, produced from Murcia to Catalonia, without forgetting the Balearic Islands. Anchovies from La Escala, vegetables from the market gardens of Levante, cold meat from Murcia, Majorca and Catalonia and much more go some way to illustrating the enormous variety of tapas to be found in the pleasant establishments of these popular tourist destinations.

available everywhere, the most popular drink here is beer. As for the different varieties of tapa, the most frequently found and typical on the coast are seafood, fish and

In the Canary Islands we can find a little of everything, as visitor demand ensures that

the basic ingredients are shipped to the archipelago to provide a full range of options. Needless to say, local delicacies also exist, such as the fantastic *papas arrugás*, wrinkly potatoes with a green or picón mojo sauce.

Aragon, La Rioja and Navarre merit a chapter apart. For one thing, all three autonomous communities produce excellent wine whilst, for another, the combination of first-class products and superb culinary skills results in a selection of tapas which, if you are not careful, can turn an aperitif into a huge, succulent banquet. Here are tiny pots of stew (*chistorra*), croquettes (*zarandajos*) and a thousand temptations more to delight the most demanding palate.

We come now to the Basque Country, where the "pintxo" is king, accompanied by a "pote" or a "chiquito" of wine, whether a good red, the typical txakolí, or even cider. The truth is that Basque bars, their counters packed with tiny delicacies, are a temptation practically impossible to resist.

Neither do Santander and Asturias have anything to envy, and the shortage of locally-produced wine is made up for by greater consumption of cider and beer. Once more, the shellfish here is of the highest quality, whilst the tiny pots of beans and potatoes will prepare the visitor formidably for a long, bracing walk through the country or along the sea front.

Reaching Galicia, with its superb Albariño and Ribeiro wine and its shellfish, the best in the world, we can enjoy delicious pasties or *empanadas*, made from "Xoubas", from bonito or even from clams, not to mention *lacón con grelos* and the unforgettable octopus dish *pulpo a feira*.

Extremadura and the two Castillas (Castilla la Nueva and Castilla la Vieja) also offer interesting variations on the theme, including the highest quality cold meats and cheeses, small portions of excellent dishes, many featuring game, such as *morteruelo conquense* and *gazpacho manchego* (which has nothing to do with the *gazpacho* made in Andalusia) and a variety of different wines, also of the highest.

Finally, we come to Madrid, where the tapa is nothing less than a cult. There are establishments offering these tasty sweetmeats all over the city, absolutely everywhere, and the visitor can also try wines of all types and from all regions in the Spanish capital, by the glass and accompanied by products and dishes from all over the country, freshly served in bars and kitchens here. And, of course, the fantastic local tapas: *tripe, patatas bravas, soldaditos de Pavía* and "marriages" of salted and fresh anchovies.

I hope and trust that this book will serve the reader as a souvenir of the fantastic world of tapas, helping him or her to make them easily for the enjoyment of family and friends.

Ángel de Miguel

VEGETABLES
AND MUSHROOMS

Ajilimójili
(Garlic and Pepper Sauce)

Ingredients for 12 people: **Difficulty:** ✴✴

✓ 1 kg potatoes
✓ 3 red peppers
✓ 3 cloves garlic

✓ ½ cup virgin olive oil
✓ Salt

Wash the potatoes and boil in salted water until tender. Peel, make purée and place in a bowl. Wash peppers, spread with oil and roast in oven with garlic; when cooked, cover with a cloth or silver paper until cool, and peel. Peel garlic.

Mix peppers and garlic into the potato purée and blend well to obtain a uniform cream. Season and add oil, beating all the time, as if making mayonnaise. Serve with toast. (Either a mortar and pestle or a mixer can be used to prepare this dish).

Recommended drink: D.O. Navarra rosé wine.

ALCACHOFAS CON ANCHOAS
(ARTICHOKES WITH ANCHOVIES)

Ingredients for 6 people: **Difficulty:** ✳✳

- ✓ 12 artichoke hearts
- ✓ 24 anchovies in oil
- ✓ 50 g serrano cured ham
- ✓ 2 sweet red peppers
- ✓ 6 tablespoonsful olive oil
- ✓ 1 tablespoonful sherry vinegar
- ✓ Salt

Slice peppers into strips and put by, then chop up the ham and sprinkle small pieces inside the cooked artichoke hearts, carefully opening them a little. Arrange standing in a serving dish. Slice anchovies lengthways and arrange two pieces crosswise over each artichoke heart.

Arrange peppers in the middle of the artichokes, then mix oil, vinegar and salt in a bowl and pour mixture over artichokes.

Recommended drink: D.O. Jerez fino sherry wine.

CANASTILLAS DE SALMOREJO
(LITTLE BASKETS OF SALMOREJO COLD SOUP)

Ingredients for 6 people: **Difficulty:** ✳✳

- ✓ 18 small tartlets
- ✓ 300 g tomato
- ✓ 2 slices bread
- ✓ 1 clove garlic
- ✓ 1 egg yolk

- ✓ 6 tablespoonsful virgin olive oil
- ✓ 2 tablespoonsful sherry vinegar
- ✓ 30 g serrano cured ham
- ✓ 1 hard-boiled egg
- ✓ Salt

Peel and chop tomatoes, place in mixer bowl with the garlic, peeled and chopped, the bread, soaked in water then drained, and the egg yolk. Add vinegar and salt, and beat to obtain a uniform cream. Add oil gradually, beating all the time, until it begins to thicken (if too thick, add a little water).

Season to taste and fill the tartlets, decorate with the ham and the hard-boiled egg, chopped, and serve immediately to ensure that the tartlets do not go soft.

Recommended drink: Beer.

CHAMPIÑONES RELLENOS
(STUFFED MUSHROOMS)

Ingredients for 8 people: **Difficulty:** ✳✳

- ✓ 400 g mushrooms
- ✓ 100 g serrano cured ham
- ✓ Parsley
- ✓ ½ lemon
- ✓ 3 tablespoonsful olive oil
- ✓ Ground pepper and salt

Cut stalks off mushrooms, leaving only the heads, and clean well under running cold water, drying with a cloth, then sprinkle with lemon to stop them from going black and put by. Pour oil into a large frying pan and, when hot, arrange mushrooms, previously seasoned, in pan, face down. Fry gently for 5 minutes.

Chop ham and parsley very fine. After 5 minutes, turn mushrooms over and stuff with ham and parsley. Cover frying pan and fry over a high flame until mushrooms are golden and ham has lost some of its fat. Serve hot.

Recommended drink: D.O. Ribera del Duero Crianza red wine.

CAZUELITAS DE PIMIENTOS DE PADRÓN
(PADRÓN PEPPERS IN DISHES)

Ingredients for 8 people: *Difficulty:* ✳

- ✓ 400 g Padrón peppers
- ✓ 150 g tomatoes
- ✓ 1 spring onion
- ✓ 6 tablespoonsful olive oil
- ✓ Salt

Wash and drain peppers well. Heat oil frying pan and fry peppers gently, turning from time to time until slightly golden. Remove, drain and add salt to taste.

Peel and chop tomatoes. Peel and chop spring onion very fine. Dress tomatoes and onion with a little oil from frying the peppers and add salt. Serve peppers hot, accompanied by the salad.

Recommended drink: D.O. Bierzo young red wine.

Emparedados de berenjenas
(Aubergine sandwiches)

Ingredients for 4 people:

Difficulty: ✳✳✳

- ✓ 2 medium-sized aubergines
- ✓ 100 g sobrasada red sausage
- ✓ 1 egg
- ✓ 2 tablespoonsful flour
- ✓ ½ cup olive oil for frying
- ✓ Salt

Wash aubergines and cut into fine slices. Leave in a bowl with salted water for 10 or 15 minutes. Drain and dry with kitchen roll. Spread each slice with a thin layer of sobrasada and join them in twos to make sandwiches, pressing the edges to make sure the filling does not come out.

Dip sandwiches in batter made from mixing egg and flour, and fry in plenty of hot oil. Drain on kitchen roll and serve hot.

Recommended drink: D.O. Pla de Bages young white wine.

Papas arrugadas
(Canary Island wrinkly potatoes)

Ingredients for 6 people: **Difficulty:** ✳✳

- ✓ ½ kg small potatoes
- ✓ 300 g rock salt
- ✓ 1 teaspoonful hot paprika
- ✓ ½ chilli pepper

- ✓ 2 cloves garlic
- ✓ ½ tablespoonful cumin
- ✓ 2 tablespoonsful wine vinegar
- ✓ 2 tablespoonsful olive oil

To prepare the potatoes ("papas"). In a pan, cover potatoes in salted water, reserving 1 tablespoonful salt for the mojo sauce, and boil. When cooked, drain, cover pan again and simmer gently, covering the lid with a cloth, until totally dry.

To prepare the mojo sauce. Peel garlic and crush in the mortar with cumin, the tablespoonful of salt put by, the chilli pepper and the paprika. Mix into a paste then add oil and vinegar, diluting a little with water (optionally, for a redder colour, add one tablespoonful fried tomato).

Recommended drink: D.O. Tacoronte-Acentejo rosé wine.

Patatas Alioli
(Potatoes in a garlic mayonnaise sauce)

Ingredients for 4 people: **Difficulty:** ✱✱

✓ 400 g potatoes   ✓ 1 cup olive oil   ✓ Salt

✓ 2 cloves garlic   ✓ Chopped parsley

Peel potatoes, wash well and place in a saucepan, covered by salted water. Boil until tender (15-30 minutes, depending on size). Drain and leave to cool.

Meanwhile, peel garlic and crush with salt in mortar to make a paste, then add oil in a thin, steady trickle, stirring all the time to bind the garlic mayonnaise sauce.

Dice potatoes and arrange in a dish. Cover with the garlic mayonnaise sauce and sprinkle with chopped parsley.

Recommended drink: Beer.

PATATAS AL CABRALES
(POTATOES IN CABRALES CHEESE)

Ingredients for 4 people: **Difficulty:** ✱

✓ 4 medium-sized potatoes   ✓ 200 g Cabrales cheese   ✓ 1 cup cream

Wash potatoes well and boil in salted water until tender.
Break up the cream and place it in a pan with the cream. Place over heat and stir with a wooden spoon until it melts.
Remove from heat and beat vigorously. Leave to rest until it thickens slightly.
Cut potatoes in half, arrange them on a serving dish and cover with the cream. Serve hot or cold, to taste.

Recommended drink: D.O. Bierzo Crianza red wine.

PATATAS BRAVAS
(POTATOES IN PAPRIKA SAUCE)

Ingredients for 8 people:

Difficulty: ✱✱

- ✓ 1 kg potatoes
- ✓ 1 tablespoonful flour
- ✓ ¼ cup vinegar
- ✓ ½ kg ripe tomatoes
- ✓ ½ teaspoonful hot paprika
- ✓ Olive oil
- ✓ Salt

Peel, chop and wash the potatoes, drying well with kitchen roll. Heat abundant oil in a pan and fry until golden. Remove and put by, hot.
Peel and chop tomato and fry in a little oil. Add vinegar, flour and paprika. Season, stir well and pour sauce over potatoes.

Recommended drink: D.O. Valdepeñas Crianza red wine.

Patatitas rellenas
(Stuffed baby potatoes)

Ingredients for 6 people: **Difficulty:** ✳✳✳

- ✓ 12 new baby potatoes
- ✓ 250 g minced beef
- ✓ 1 tablespoonful breadcrumbs
- ✓ 1 clove garlic
- ✓ 1 tablespoonful chopped parsley

- ✓ 1 tablespoonful white wine
- ✓ 2 eggs
- ✓ 2 tablespoonsful flour
- ✓ ¾ cups olive oil
- ✓ 1 small onion

- ✓ Saffron
- ✓ Ground pepper
- ✓ 1 cup stock
- ✓ Salt

Peel and wash the potatoes, carefully removing pulp with a spoon, leaving a hole for the stuffing. Beat an egg in a bowl, season and add meat, breadcrumbs, garlic and chopped parsley; stir well and fill the holes in the potatoes. Dip meat part in flour and the rest of the beaten egg. Heat oil in a deep frying pan and fry potatoes until lightly golden.

Pour 3 tablespoonsful oil into an earthenware bowl and lightly fry the chopped onion. Once transparent, add potatoes, wine, stock, saffron, salt and pepper. Cover and simmer until the potatoes are tender, around 20-30 minutes. Serve hot.

Recommended drink: Crianza D.O. Priorat red wine.

ROLLITOS DE PIMIENTO
(PEPPER ROLLS)

Ingredients for 6 people: **Difficulty:** ✳✳

- ✓ 3 large sweet red pimento peppers
- ✓ 100 g tuna fish in oil
- ✓ 1 cup mayonnaise
- ✓ 1 gherkin, chopped
- ✓ The breadcrumbs from 1 slice of bread
- ✓ 1 tablespoonful white wine
- ✓ ¼ lettuce, chopped
- ✓ 50 g green olives
- ✓ Salt

Wash and drain liquid from peppers and slice each into four pieces.
Mix the tuna, the mayonnaise, the gherkin, finely chopped, the bread and the wine in a blender or the mortar. Season to taste.
Arrange the slices of pepper on a flat surface and cover each with one teaspoonful of the tuna fish paste. Turn them into rolls and arrange them around a serving dish or side plates. Arrange the olives and the lettuce in the centre.

Recommended drink: D.O. Ribera del Guadiana young red wine.

PIMIENTOS RELLENOS DE MORCILLA
(STUFFED PEPPERS WITH MORCILLA BLACK PUDDING)

Ingredients for 4 people: **Difficulty:** ✱✱✱

- ✓ 8 preserved piquillo peppers
- ✓ 200 g onion morcilla black pudding
- ✓ 1 onion
- ✓ 2 tablespoonsful flour
- ✓ 1 cup milk
- ✓ 4 tablespoonsful olive oil
- ✓ 1 tablespoonful butter
- ✓ 2 tablespoonsful fried tomato
- ✓ 1 tablespoonful chopped parsley
- ✓ Ground pepper
- ✓ Salt

Pour liquid from peppers and put both liquid and peppers by for later. Chop onion very fine and break up black pudding. Heat butter with 1 tablespoonful oil and lightly fry 1/3 of the onion until transparent. Add flour and stir well. Pour in milk stirring all the time and simmer for a few minutes. Add the meat from the morcilla, season and stir well. Leave on a plate to cool. Stuff the peppers with the morcilla béchamel and place in an ovenproof dish. Heat the rest of the oil and lightly fry the remaining onion until it begins to turn golden. Add 2 tablespoonsful of the liquid from the peppers, the fried tomato, salt and pepper. Pour over peppers and bake in oven for 15-20 minutes a 130°. Sprinkle with chopped parsley and serve with accompaniment to taste.
Recommended drink: D.O. Rioja Crianza red wine.

Ensaladilla rusa
(Potato salad)

Ingredients for 4 people:

Difficulty: ✷✷

- ✓ 500 g potatoes
- ✓ 50 g peas
- ✓ 50 g green beans
- ✓ 50 g carrots
- ✓ 100 g tuna in oil
- ✓ 1 morrón pepper
- ✓ 1 hard-boiled egg
- ✓ 2 tablespoonsful olive oil
- ✓ ½ teaspoonful vinegar or lemon
- ✓ 1 cup mayonnaise
- ✓ Salt

Peel, wash and cut the potatoes into small cubes, then boil in salted water. Do the same with the other vegetables, draining well.

Put the potatoes into a wide dish, add carrots, peas, beans and tuna fish, crumbled, and stir well.

Sprinkle with olive oil and vinegar or lemon. Add mayonnaise and season with salt to taste, mixing well.

Arrange the potato salad on a serving plate, decorate with pepper, cut into strips and the hard-boiled egg, sliced. Store in the fridge until serving.

Recommended drink: D.O. Moriles fino sherry wine.

TOMATITOS RELLENOS
(STUFFED CHERRY TOMATOES)

Ingredients for 6 people:

Difficulty: ✳

✓ 12 cherry tomatoes (not too small)
✓ 1 egg
✓ ¼ cup cream
✓ 2 tablespoonsful grated cheese

✓ 1 tablespoonful breadcrumbs
✓ Ground pepper
✓ Nutmeg
✓ Salt

Wash the cherry tomatoes, dry and cut off top. Remove pulp, being careful not to break the tomatoes and place them on a plate, face down. In a bowl, whip the egg, season and add the nutmeg, the cheese, the breadcrumbs and the cream. Stir well and leave to rest for a few minutes to allow the bread to become spongy. Stuff the tomatoes with this mixture and place on a baking tray. Bake for 8-10 minutes at 200°, or until the stuffing is cooked. Serve immediately.

Recommended drink: D.O. Bullas white wine Crianza.

PISTO MANCHEGO
(LA MANCHA STYLE RATATOUILLE)

Ingredients for 10 people: **Difficulty:** ✱✱✱

✓ 500 g tomato   ✓ 2 green peppers
✓ 500 g courgettes   ✓ 6 tablespoonsful olive oil
✓ 1 large onion   ✓ Salt
✓ 1 red pepper

Peel and chop tomatoes, wash peppers, remove seeds and chop. Wash and chop courgettes. Heat oil in a large frying pan or saucepan and lightly fry the onion, peeled and chopped. When the onion is transparent, add the peppers, turn over once or twice and add courgettes. Stir well and simmer for 6 or 7 minutes.
When the vegetables are completely fried, add tomato, simmer for 30 minutes, stirring frequently to ensure it does not stick. Season and serve hot, in individual dishes or on small pieces of toast.

Recommended drink: D.O. Rueda Crianza white wine.

Setas rellenas
(Stuffed mushrooms)

Ingredients for 6 people:

- ✓ 12 Niscaló mushrooms
- ✓ 1 large onion
- ✓ 2 slices bread
- ✓ 1 lemon
- ✓ 2 tablespoonsful grated cheese
- ✓ 1 tablespoonful chopped parsley
- ✓ Ground pepper
- ✓ 5 tablespoonsful olive oil
- ✓ Salt

Difficulty: ✳✳

Wash the mushrooms, removing any earthy parts. Cut off stalks and chop. Peel and chop the onion. Grate the lemon peel and squeeze lemon.

Heat 3 tablespoonsful oil in a frying pan and lightly fry the onion and mushroom stalks. Season with salt and pepper and fry until tender and juice is reduced.

Remove frying pan from heat, crumble bread and add to mixture, along with 3 table-spoonsful lemon juice, 1 tablespoonful grated lemon, the grated cheese and the chopped parsley. Stir well.

Grease mushrooms with oil stuff with the mixture. Arrange on an ovenproof dish and place in preheated oven. Bake for 15-20 minutes at high temperature (200°).

Recommended drink: D.O. Priorat Crianza red wine.

BERENJENAS CON MIEL
(AUBERGINES WITH HONEY)

Ingredients for 6 people:

Difficulty: ✴✴

- ✓ 1 aubergine
- ✓ ½ cup flour
- ✓ 4 tablespoonsful sugar syrup
- ✓ 2 cups lemonade or soda
- ✓ 1 cup olive oil
- ✓ Salt

Peel aubergine, cut into rough slices, then cut slices into strips. Place aubergine strips in a bowl and add salt and lemonade soda, leaving it to rest for 30-40 minutes.
Drain well, dip in flour and fry in plenty of hot oil until slightly golden. Drain on kitchen roll. Serve the aubergine strips hot, covered with syrup.

Recommended drink: D.O. Moriles fino sherry wine.

FRITURAS DE COLIFLOR
(CAULIFLOWER FRITTERS)

Ingredients for 8 people: **Difficulty: ✷✷**

- ✓ 750 g cauliflower
- ✓ 2 eggs
- ✓ 2 tablespoonful cornflour
- ✓ 1 cup tomato sauce
- ✓ 3 tablespoonsful milk
- ✓ 50 g butter
- ✓ 1 tablespoonful breadcrumbs
- ✓ 1 tablespoonful grated cheese
- ✓ Ground black pepper
- ✓ Olive oil
- ✓ Salt

Cut the cauliflower up into fairly small sprigs, wash and boil in salted water until "al dente". Drain well.

Beat eggs in a deep plate, add cornflour, dissolved in milk, salt, pepper and stir well until a thick cream forms. Heat plenty of oil in a frying pan. Dip the cauliflower sprigs in the batter and fry in hot oil. Drain well and arrange in a serving dish.

In a saucepan, mix the tomato sauce, the cheese, the butter and the breadcrumbs. Simmer for a minute or two, stirring with a wooden spoon, and serve separately in a sauce or gravy boat to accompany the cauliflower.

Recommended drink: D.O. La Mancha young white wine.

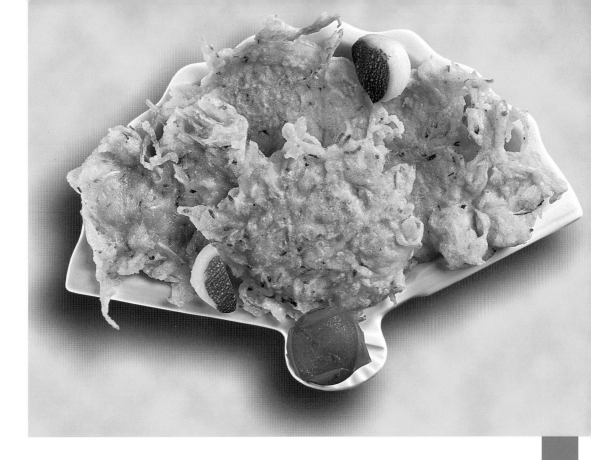

TORTITAS DE VERDURAS
(VEGETABLE FRITTERS)

Ingredients for 6 people: **Difficulty:** ✳✳✳

- ✓ 300 g courgettes
- ✓ 1 spring onion
- ✓ 300 g carrots
- ✓ 150 g cabbage
- ✓ 6 tablespoonsful flour
- ✓ 2 eggs
- ✓ Ground pepper
- ✓ Olive oil for frying
- ✓ Salt

Wash all the vegetables and cut into thin slices. Mix flour and eggs together and season.
Add the vegetables to the flour and egg mixture and stir well, mixing all the ingredients together.
Heat plenty of oil in a frying pan and pour in tablespoonsful of the mixture, pressing them lightly down and frying at a moderate heat. Turn once until crunchy and golden on either side, 3 or 4 minutes each. Drain on kitchen roll and serve.

Recommended drink: D.O. Navarra rosé wine.

FISH AND SHELLFISH

ALMEJAS A LA ESPAÑOLA
(SPANISH STYLE CLAMS)

Ingredients for 4 people: **Difficulty:** ✳✳

- ✓ 750 g clams
- ✓ ½ small onion
- ✓ 2 cloves garlic
- ✓ 1 ½ tablespoonful flour
- ✓ ¼ cup white wine

- ✓ ½ tablespoonful sweet paprika
- ✓ Parsley
- ✓ 3 tablespoonsful olive oil
- ✓ ¼ cup water
- ✓ Salt

Wash the clams, drain and put by. Peel and chop the onion and garlic.
Heat oil in a pan and lightly fry garlic and onion until transparent. Mix in chopped parsley, stir a little and add paprika and flour; stir with a wooden spoon and pour in wine.
Add clams and water. Cover and simmer until clams open. Add salt to taste and serve immediately.

Recommended drink: D.O. Penedés young white wine.

ALMEJAS RELLENAS
(STUFFED CLAMS)

Ingredients for 4 people: **Difficulty:** ✷✷

- ✓ 750 g clams
- ✓ 50 g serrano cured ham
- ✓ 1 small onion
- ✓ 1 tablespoonful chopped parsley
- ✓ 2 tablespoonsful olive oil
- ✓ 1 tablespoonful flour
- ✓ 1 tablespoonful breadcrumbs
- ✓ 1 egg yolk
- ✓ Ground pepper and salt

Soak clams in cold, salted water for one hour. Open by heating in a pan with a few tablespoonsful water, drain off stock and put by. Remove clams from shells, and chop.
Heat oil in a frying pan and lightly fry the chopped onion on a low heat until; add ham, chopped, and flour and lightly fry for a few minutes, stirring all the time. Add chopped clams, stock and parsley; stir, season and simmer until a thick cream forms. Remove from heat, add egg yolk and stir. Stuff clam shells with this creamy mixture.
Place on an oven dish, sprinkle with bread-crumbs, gratinate and serve immediately.

Recommended drink: D.O. Jerez young white wine.

BARQUITAS DE ENDIBIAS CON SALMÓN
(ENDIVE AND SALMON BARQUETTES)

Ingredients for 8 people: **Difficulty:** ✳

✓ 4 endives
✓ 200 g smoked salmon
✓ 50 g cooked prawns, peeled
✓ 1 cup mayonnaise

✓ 1 spring onion
✓ 1 teaspoonful mustard
✓ 2 tablespoonsful lemon juice

Remove the outside leaves from the endives, wash, dry and put by.
In a bowl, stir mayonnaise together with mustard and lemon juice.
Chop spring onion and endive hearts and mix with prawns, half the sliced salmon and the mustard and mayonnaise sauce.
Stuff the endive leaves you put by with this mixture, decorating with a little salmon left over. Place in fridge for a while and serve cold.

Recommended drink: D.O. Penedés Crianza white wine.

CHIPIRONES EN SU TINTA
(SQUID IN THEIR INK)

Ingredients for 8 people: **Difficulty:** ✳✳✳

✓ 16 squid   ✓ 1 green pepper   ✓ 3 tablespoonsful olive oil

✓ 1 large onion   ✓ 2 tomatoes   ✓ Salt

✓ 2 cloves garlic   ✓ 1 cup fish stock

Clean squid well, removing tentacles and ink sac.
Heat oil in a frying pan and lightly fry half onion and 1 clove garlic, finely chopped.
When they start to become golden, add squid tentacles and stir with a wooden spoon.
Drain off excess oil, add salt to taste and stuff squid with this mixture, closing up the opening with a cocktail stick.
Fry remaining garlic in oil used to fry onion and quickly fry squid and put by.
Lightly fry remaining onion in a pan with pepper and tomatoes, chopped, for around 20 minutes. Add stock and squid ink, stirring well. Add squid and simmer until sauce thickens. Accompany with fried bread.

Recommended drink: D.O. Madrid Crianza red wine.

BOQUERONES CON PICADILLO
(ANCHOVIES WITH PICADILLO SAUCE)

Ingredients for 8 people: **Difficulty:** ✳✳

- ✓ 500 g small anchovies
- ✓ 1 pepper
- ✓ 1 medium-sized onion
- ✓ 2 tomatoes
- ✓ 100 g flour

- ✓ 1 tablespoonful sherry vinegar
- ✓ 2 tablespoonsful virgin olive oil
- ✓ Olive oil for frying
- ✓ Salt

Wash pepper and tomatoes, and peel onion; place the vegetables on oven tray, sprinkle with oil and bake. Peel pepper and tomatoes, chop all and add a little oil, vinegar and salt, mixing well; put by.
Wash and drain anchovies well, lightly season, dip in flour and fry in plenty of hot oil. Drain on kitchen roll and serve immediately with picadillo.

Recommended drink: D.O. Jerez fino sherry wine.

BOQUERONES EN VINAGRE
(ANCHOVIES IN VINEGAR)

Ingredients for 12 people:

Difficulty: ✶✶

✓ 1 kg anchovies

✓ 1 sprig parsley

✓ 2 cups water

✓ 1 cup wine vinegar

✓ ½ cup virgin olive oil

✓ 2 cloves garlic

✓ 2 tablespoonsful rock salt

Wash anchovies and remove heads, insides and backbone, leaving the fillets whole. Wash in cold water until water stays clear. Freeze for 24 hours, then defreeze.

Place in a dish, forming layers, covering with brine made from the salt and 2 cups water. Leave for 3 hours in a cool place. Drain, place in a bowl with the skin up and cover with vinegar and ½ cup water; leave for 3-4 hours, until very white. Remove from vinegar, drain well, arrange in dish and sprinkle with oil. Sprinkle with finely-chopped garlic and parsley. Accompany with olives.

Recommended drink: Beer.

BOQUERONES AL AJILLO
(ANCHOVIES IN GARLIC)

Ingredients for 8 people:

Difficulty: ✳✳

- ✓ 500 g anchovies
- ✓ 4 cloves garlic
- ✓ 8 tablespoonsful olive oil
- ✓ ½ cup white wine
- ✓ 3 tablespoonsful vinegar
- ✓ 1 sprig parsley
- ✓ Chilli pepper
- ✓ Salt

Remove anchovy heads and insides and carefully open in two to remove backbone. Wash well in cold water and leave to soak for 10 minutes. Remove from water and drain in a plate on kitchen roll.

Peel garlic and cut into thin slices. Heat oil in a frying pan until it begins to smoke, add garlic and chilli pepper, frying until garlic is golden. Remove chilli pepper and put by.

Place anchovies in frying pan and fry for a minute or two. Pour in wine and vinegar and move frying pan around for about 2 minutes on a low heat until the anchovies are done. Season.

Turn up heat and simmer for just a few minutes until the liquid evaporates a little. Remove pan from heat and sprinkle anchovies with chopped parsley.

Recommended drink: D.O. Albariño young white wine.

Boquerones con sorpresa
(Anchovies surprise)

Ingredients for 8 people: **Difficulty:** ✳✳✳

- ✓ 500 g anchovies
- ✓ 3 sweet red pimento peppers, baked and peeled
- ✓ 1 egg
- ✓ 2 tablespoonsful flour
- ✓ Olive oil
- ✓ Salt

Clean anchovies, remove heads and wash under running cold water. Dry and carefully open in two to remove backbone. Lightly salt.
Cut peppers into thin strips. Take each anchovy in the hand, place a strip of pepper instead of the backbone, and close again.
Dip anchovies in flour and then in the beaten egg.
Heat plenty of oil in a frying pan and fry anchovies until golden. Remove, drain on kitchen roll and serve immediately.

Recommended drink: D.O. Jumilla young red wine.

Brandada de Bacalao
(Cod brandade)

Ingredients for 8 people:

Difficulty: ✳✳

✓ 200 g salted cod

✓ 10 tablespoonful olive oil

✓ 750 g potatoes

✓ 2 cloves garlic

Place cod in pan with cold water and leave to soak for 24-36 hours, according to thickness; change water 3 times. Boil the peeled potatoes for 20 minutes or until tender, then add cod and simmer for 2-3 minutes, until the fish strips begin to separate. Drain, putting by a little of the liquid from cooking.

In a large mortar, crush garlic and add potatoes, one by one, crushing and stirring all the time. Crumble up the cod, add it to the potatoes and add oil, stirring all the time. If it is too thick, add a little of the cooking liquid you put by to make an even pure. Serve with rounds of toast.

Recommended drink: D.O. Costers del Segre Crianza red wine.

BUÑUELOS DE BACALAO
(COD FRITTERS)

Ingredients for 4 people:

Difficulty: ✱✱

- ✓ 150 g crumbled cod
- ✓ 1 cup beer
- ✓ 1 spring onion
- ✓ 2 tablespoonsful chopped parsley
- ✓ 150 g flour
- ✓ ¼ cup olive oil for frying
- ✓ Salt

Put the crumbled cod into a bowl. Cover with cold water and leave to soak for 15-20 minutes. Remove cod and drain well.

Pour beer into a wide bowl. Gradually add flour and salt and stir well, using a hand whisk. Make a smooth paste, then add finely-chopped onion and parsley. Stir again, and add drained cod. Stir.

Heat plenty of oil in a frying pan; when hot, use spoon to scoop up portions of the paste and place in oil. Fry until golden. Drain on kitchen roll and serve with slices of lemon.

Recommended drink: D.O. Valdepeñas Crianza red wine.

CALAMARES A LA ROMANA
(SQUID FRIED IN BATTER)

Ingredients for 6 people: **Difficulty: ✳✳**

- ✓ 500 g squid
- ✓ 1 lemon
- ✓ 1 egg
- ✓ ½ cup milk
- ✓ 6 tablespoonsful flour
- ✓ ½ small teaspoonful yeast in powder
- ✓ ½ cup olive oil for frying
- ✓ Salt

Clean and wash squid thoroughly. Remove heads and tentacles, cut into rings and dry with kitchen roll. Pour flour and yeast into a bowl, add salt and the egg, beaten, and the milk, little by little, stirring well all the time, to make a smooth, thick batter.

Heat plenty of oil in a deep frying pan. When it starts to smoke, dip rings in batter and place in boiling oil. Turning once, fry until golden on both sides, remove and place on kitchen roll to drain excess oil. Arrange squid in a serving dish, decorate with lemon slices and serve.

Recommended drink: Beer.

Cangrejos en salsa
(Crab in sauce)

Ingredients for 6 people:

Difficulty: ✹✹✹

- ✓ 1 kg de river crabs
- ✓ 1 large onion
- ✓ 50 g serrano cured ham
- ✓ 1 chilli pepper
- ✓ 1 cup dry white wine
- ✓ 7 tablespoonsful olive oil
- ✓ 500 g fresh tomatoes, chopped
- ✓ 1 tablespoonful chopped parsley
- ✓ Salt

To prepare crabs: grasp the centre of the tail and pull to remove the bitter part. Wash well and drain. Heat half the oil and fry the tomato to obtain a thick sauce, then heat the rest of the oil in a frying pan and fry crabs until they change colour. Remove, drain and place in a saucepan.

Peel the onion, chop fine, and fry in the same oil as the crabs until transparent. Add the ham, chopped and the chilli pepper to the saucepan. Stir, then add wine, tomato and crabs, and season. Cover, simmer for around 5 minutes, sprinkle with chopped parsley and serve.

Recommended drink: D.O. Rioja Crianza red wine.

ROLLITOS DE SALMÓN Y QUESO
(SALMON AND CHEESE ROLLS)

Ingredients for 8 people: **Difficulty:** ✳

- ✓ 250 g smoked salmon
- ✓ 250 g creamy cheese
- ✓ 1 tablespoonful lemon juice
- ✓ 1 spring small onion

- ✓ 1 bunch chives
- ✓ 3 tablespoonsful extra virgin olive oil
- ✓ 1 teaspoonful mustard
- ✓ Ground pepper and salt

Cut smoked salmon into rectangular pieces. Peel spring onion and chop very fine. Wash and chop chives. Place cheese in a bowl and add spring onion, chives, mustard, 1 tablespoonful oil, salt and pepper. Stir well and leave in fridge for 1 hour.
Spread salmon pieces over a worktop and spread the cheese mix over them. Roll them up and place rolls in a dish. Sprinkle with the remaining oil just before serving.

Recommended drink: D.O. Bullas Crianza white wine.

Croquetas de gambas
(Prawn croquettes)

Ingredients for 8 people:

Difficulty: ✱✱✱

- ✓ 500 g prawns
- ✓ 2 hard-boiled eggs
- ✓ 2 tablespoonsful butter
- ✓ 150 g flour
- ✓ ¾ litre milk
- ✓ 2 eggs
- ✓ 50 g breadcrumbs
- ✓ Olive oil
- ✓ Salt

Peel prawns and fry heads and shells in 2 tablespoonsful oil. Remove, drain and add butter; once melted, add flour, stir and add milk little by little, stirring all the time with a wooden spoon to make a béchamel sauce.

Add prawns, peeled and hard-boiled eggs, all chopped. Bring to boil, season and pour into a dish. Leave to cool.

Make the croquettes, dip in eggs, beaten, and breadcrumbs. Fry in plenty of hot oil, drain on kitchen roll and serve.

Recommended drink: D.O. Txakolí de Vizcaya young white wine.

EMPANADILLAS DE ATÚN
(TUNAFISH PASTIES)

Ingredients for 4 people:　　　　　　　　　　　　　　　　**Difficulty:** ✳✳✳

- ✓ 250 g flour
- ✓ ¼ cup white wine
- ✓ 1 pinch bicarbonate
- ✓ 200 g tunafish in oil
- ✓ ½ cup fried tomato
- ✓ 1 egg
- ✓ Olive oil
- ✓ Salt

To prepare the dough. Pour flour into a bowl to form a volcano. Pour the wine into the crater, along with ¼ cup oil, salt and bicarbonate. Stir to form a mass and knead for a while with the hands. Leave to rest for around 30 minutes.

To prepare the filling. Crumble tuna fish and mix with tomato and egg, peeled and finely chopped.

Sprinkle flour over the worktop, spread dough out with a roller, and place little mounds of the dough over this mass. Cut dough into circles using a knife or a glass and fold each up, pressing the edges together with a fork. Heat plenty of oil in a frying pan and fry the pasties until golden. Drain on kitchen roll and serve.

Recommended drink: Crianza red wine D.O. La Mancha.

FRITURA A LA ANDALUZA
(ANDALUSIAN FRIED SEAFOOD)

Ingredients for 10 people: **Difficulty:** ✱✱

✓ 350 g anchovies
✓ 350 g squid
✓ 350 g puntillitas (small squid)

✓ 400 g red mullet
✓ 3 tablespoonsful special flour for frying
✓ ¼ cup olive oil for frying and salt

Wash the small squid, the mullet, the anchovies and the squid, cut into rings. Wash and drain well, season slightly and dip in flour, shaking to remove any excess flour.
Heat plenty of olive oil in a frying pan and fry fish in batches, ensuring that the oil does not cool. Once golden, drain on kitchen roll and serve immediately.

Recommended drink: D.O. Jerez fino sherry wine.

Gambas al Ajillo
(Prawns in garlic)

Ingredients for 4 people: **Difficulty:** ✳

- ✓ 250 g peeled prawns
- ✓ 3 tablespoonsful olive oil
- ✓ 1 chilli pepper

- ✓ 3 cloves garlic
- ✓ Salt

Peel garlic, cut into slices and place in earthenware or ovenproof dishes with cold oil and chilli pepper.
Heat, and when garlic is golden add prawns and salt. Stir, cover and turn off heat to complete cooking. Serve hot.

Recommended drink: D.O. Rioja young red wine.

LANGOSTINOS CON GUACAMOLE
(PRAWNS WITH GUACAMOLE)

Ingredients for 4 people: **Difficulty:** ✳

- ✓ 1 avocado
- ✓ 200 g langostino prawns
- ✓ ½ small onion
- ✓ 1 small tomato
- ✓ 2 tablespoonsful chopped coriander

- ✓ ½ lemon
- ✓ 2 tablespoonsful olive oil
- ✓ 1 pinch tabasco
- ✓ Ground pepper
- ✓ Salt

Cut avocado in half lengthways, remove stone and mash pulp with a fork to make purée. Add the onion and tomato, both grated, the chopped coriander, the lemon juice, salt, pepper, 1 tablespoonful oil and the tabasco. Mix well.
Peel the langostino prawns and fry in a frying pan or grille in the remaining oil, turning once. Serve guacamole on Chinese spoons or on tartlets with a whole or half prawn on each.

Recommended drink: Beer.

LANGOSTINOS EN GABARDINA
(PASTRY COATED PRAWNS)

Ingredients for 4 people: **Difficulty: ✳✳**

- ✓ 500 g langostino prawns
- ✓ 1 glass beer
- ✓ 40 g flour
- ✓ ¼ teaspoonful powdered saffron
- ✓ ¾ cup olive oil
- ✓ Salt

Peel prawns, leaving shell at the end of tail. Pour beer into a bowl and add saffron and salt. Add flour little by little to form a smooth, thick cream, enough to cover the prawn tails. Heat plenty of oil in a deep frying pan, dip prawns in batter and fry in batches until golden. Drain on kitchen roll and serve hot.

Recommended drink: D.O. Penedés young white wine.

MEJILLONES CON ALIOLI
(MUSSELS IN A GARLIC MAYONNAISE SAUCE)

Ingredients for 8 people: *Difficulty:* ✳

✓ 1 ½ kg mussels   ✓ 1 clove garlic

✓ 1 cup mayonnaise   ✓ Chopped parsley

Clean mussels, well, scraping them under the cold tap. Place in a pan, cover and cook until the shells open. Remove mussels from shells and arrange in a dish.
Mix mayonnaise sauce with finely chopped garlic and parsley. Spread over mussels and serve.

Recommended drink: D.O. Vino Espumoso Brut Cava.

MEJILLONES EN VINAGRETA
(MUSSELS IN A VINAIGRETTE SAUCE)

Ingredients for 6 people: **Difficulty:** ✱

- ✓ 1 kg mussels
- ✓ 1 green pepper
- ✓ ½ onion

- ✓ 4 tablespoonsful olive oil
- ✓ 1 tablespoonful wine vinegar
- ✓ 2 tomatoes and salt

Wash mussels under the tap, scraping well with a knife to remove all dirt and algae. Place mussels in a saucepan with half cup water. Cover and heat until they open.

Finely chop tomatoes, pepper and onion. Pour into a bowl and dress with oil, vinegar and salt, mixing well.

Open mussels, remove from shell and arrange in a dish. Sprinkle vinaigrette sauce over mussels and serve.

Recommended drink: Beer.

MEJILLONES FRITOS
(FRIED MUSSELS)

Ingredients for 8 people:

Difficulty: ✱✱

- ✓ 1 ½ kg mussels
- ✓ 1 cup beer
- ✓ ¾ cup flour
- ✓ ½ lemon
- ✓ Olive oil for frying
- ✓ Salt

Clean mussels, well, scraping them under the cold tap. Place in a pan, cover and cook until the shells open. Remove mussels from shells and place on kitchen roll to drain thoroughly. Pour flour into a bowl and add beer little by little, stirring all the time, to obtain a thick cream. Add salt to taste and lemon juice, and stir.

Heat plenty of oil in a frying pan. Thread mussels on wooden cocktail sticks, two to each, dip in cream and fry in hot oil until golden. Remove, drain, and serve accompanied by yoghurt and garlic sauce, tarator sauce (ground walnuts, garlic, lemon juice and oil), etc.

Recommended drink: D.O. Valdeorras young white wine.

TIGRES
("TIGERS")

Ingredients for 8 people: **Difficulty:** ✳ ✳ ✳

✓ 1 kg mussels   ✓ 1 egg   ✓ ½ cup olive oil
✓ 2 tablespoonsful fried tomato ✓ 3 tablespoonsful breadcrumbs ✓ Ground pepper
✓ 1 cup béchamel   ✓ 1 slice bread, crumbled   ✓ Salt

Clean mussels, well, scraping them under the cold tap. Place in a pan, cover and cook until the shells open. Remove mussels from shells, chop, arrange in a bowl and add breadcrumbs, tomato, salt and pepper; stir well. Stuff mussel shells halfway, then cover with béchamel sauce.

Beat egg in a deep plate and dip mussels firstly in egg and then in breadcrumbs. Heat plenty of oil in a frying pan and fry mussels until golden. Drain on kitchen roll and serve hot.

Recommended drink: D.O. Penedés rosé wine.

Ostras al horno
(Baked oysters)

Ingredients for 6 people: **Difficulty:** ✳✳✳

- ✓ 12 oysters
- ✓ 3 tomatoes
- ✓ 2 tablespoonsful olive oil
- ✓ 1 tablespoonful chopped parsley
- ✓ 1 cup breadcrumbs
- ✓ Ground pepper
- ✓ 2 tablespoonsful butter
- ✓ Salt

Open oysters, remove from shells and boil in their juice, with a little water if necessary, for 1 minute. Remove from water and slice.
Peel and finely chop tomatoes. Heat oil in a frying pan and lightly fry tomatoes for 15-20 minutes. Add oysters, parsley, salt and pepper, stir well and boil for 1 minute more.
Spread butter on shells and stuff with the sauce.
Sprinkle with breadcrumbs and grill in preheated oven for a few minutes, until golden. Serve immediately.

Recommended drink: D.O. Rías Baixas Crianza white wine.

Pulpo a feira
(Galician style octopus)

Ingredients for 6 people:		Difficulty: ✶✶
✓ 500 g octopus	✓ 500 g small potatoes	✓ Rock salt
✓ Hot paprika	✓ 8 tablespoonsful extra virgin olive oil	
✓ ½ tablespoonful sweet paprika	✓ 2 bay leaves	

Wash octopus and dry with kitchen roll. Freeze to make tender so that we do not need to beat it. Defreeze.

Boil a saucepan full of water, with salt and bay leaf. Dip octopus several times into this water, tentacles down, finally leaving it in the water when it boils. Simmer for 30 or 40 minutes. Prick once or twice to ensure that it is tender. Remove octopus from water, drain and leave to rest for 15 minutes to allow the skin to be removed.

Peel and boil potatoes, whole or sliced, in the liquid from cooking the octopus, until tender. Slice octopus tentacles and arrange on one or more wooden platters, sprinkle with both hot and sweet paprika, and rock salt. Sprinkle evenly oil and serve warm or cold.

Recommended drink: D.O. Ribeiro young white wine.

CHOPITOS FRITOS
(FRIED SMALL SQUID)

Ingredients for 6 people: **Difficulty:** ✴✴

- ✓ 500 g chopitos (small squid)
- ✓ 6 tablespoonsful special flour for frying
- ✓ 1 cup olive oil for frying
- ✓ 1 lemon
- ✓ Salt

Wash squid well, leaving them whole. Lightly salt and place in a vegetable colander. Still in the colander, dust them with special flour for frying fish, shaking to make sure they are evenly covered and to remove any excess flour.

Heat plenty of oil in a deep frying pan and fry squid in batches until done. Drain on kitchen roll and serve immediately with lemon quarters.

Recommended drink: D.O. Jerez fino sherry wine.

Cocas de anchoas
(Anchovies on coca bread)

Ingredients for 4 people: **Difficulty:** ✳✳

- ✓ 250 g flour
- ✓ ½ cup water
- ✓ 12 anchovies
- ✓ 3 cloves garlic

- ✓ 1 tablespoonful chopped parsley
- ✓ 3 tablespoonsful olive oil
- ✓ Salt

Pour flour into a bowl and knead together with the oil, water and salt to obtain an even dough that does not stick to the hands (if necessary, add a little more flour). Then make small tarts, about 1 cm thick and arrange on the oven tray. Bake at medium temperature for 10 minutes.

Next, remove from oven and arrange anchovies, garlic and chopped parsley on top. Return to oven and bake until crisp and cold. Serve hot or cold.

Recommended drink: Beer.

RIN-RAN

Ingredients for 8 people: **Difficulty:** ✳✳

✓ 200 g salted cod   ✓ 2 cloves garlic   ✓ 8 tablespoonsful olive oil

✓ 500 g tomatoes   ✓ 50 g black olives   ✓ Salt

✓ 3 green peppers   ✓ ½ teaspoonful sugar

Soak cod for 24 hours, changing water several times.
Clean off skin and bones, drain and crumble. Heat cod in a saucepan with oil. Stir-fry for a few seconds, then add peppers, sliced, and the garlic, chopped, frying everything together for a few minutes.
Add tomatoes, chopped, sugar, season, and continue to fry gently. When everything is cooked (about 40 minutes), add olives and stir. Serve hot or cold.

Recommended drink: D.O. Rueda Crianza white wine.

EMPAREDADOS DE SARDINAS
(SARDINE TURNOVERS)

Ingredients for 12 people: **Difficulty:** ✳✳

- ✓ 1 kg medium-sized sardines
- ✓ 8 slices processed cheese
- ✓ 4 slices serrano cured ham
- ✓ 400 g potatoes

- ✓ 500 g tomatoes
- ✓ 1 onion
- ✓ 2 cloves garlic
- ✓ Parsley

- ✓ Oregano
- ✓ 10 tablespoonsful olive oil
- ✓ Ground pepper
- ✓ Salt

Open the sardines lengthways and remove scales and bones. Wash and dry.
Peel and slice potatoes and onion. Heat plenty of oil in a frying pan and fry onion and potatoes gently until slightly tender; drain and arrange in a ovenproof dish. Season.
In the mortar, grind garlic with herbs and salt to taste. Mix with tomatoes, peeled and chopped.
Arrange half the sardines, open, on a board, cover with a layer of tomato, a piece of ham, and cheese. Cover with another sardine to make "sandwich fillings". Place over potatoes and cover with the rest of the tomato. Heat oven and bake sardines at 180° for 20-25 minutes.

Recommended drink: D.O. Sanlúcar de Barrameda fino manzanilla sherry wine.

TARTITAS DE SARDINAS
(SARDINE TARTLETS)

Ingredients for 4 people:

Difficulty: ✶✶

- ✓ 4 pasta wafers for small turnovers
- ✓ 350 g small sardines
- ✓ 400 g tomatoes
- ✓ 2 cloves garlic
- ✓ 15 g sugar
- ✓ ½ cup virgin olive oil
- ✓ Oregano
- ✓ Thyme and salt

Scald tomatoes, peel and place, whole, in a pan with 1 tablespoonful oil, salt, sugar and thyme. Cover and simmer gently until cooked and soft. Put by.

Clean sardines, wash, remove head and bones and separate the fillets. Peel and chop garlic. Heat 2 tablespoonsful oil in a frying pan and fry garlic gently until golden. Add sardines, mix with oil, salt, cover and when it begins to boil, remove from heat and put by.

Fry pasta wafers in plenty of hot oil, drain well and make the tartlets by placing open tomatoes, sardine fillets on top, sprinkling with oregano. Serve hot or cold.

Recommended drink: D.O. Albariño young white wine.

EMPANADILLAS DE TRUCHA
(TROUT PASTRIES)

Ingredients for 8 people:

Difficulty: ✳✳✳

- ✓ 350 g trout
- ✓ 1 hard-boiled egg
- ✓ 1 medium-sized onion
- ✓ 1 cup olive oil
- ✓ 400 g flour
- ✓ 1/3 cup white wine
- ✓ 1/3 cup water
- ✓ Salt

To prepare the dough. Pour flour into a bowl to form a volcano, pour in wine, water and the same volume of oil; add salt and knead to form a smooth mass. Sprinkle the worktop with flour and use some of this dough to form a ball.

To prepare the filling. Wash the trout, fry in pan with oil, remove skin and bones, and crumble. Peel and chop onion, fry in 2 tablespoonsful oil and mix with trout and egg, chopped. Remove from heat and leave to cool.

Sprinkle worktop and roll out dough, use a glass to cut out circles and spread filling in the middle of each. Close circles to make the pasties and seal using a fork. Fry in hot oil, drain and serve.

Recommended drink: D.O. Penedés Crianza white wine.

Soldaditos de Pavía
(Cod fritters)

Ingredients for 8 people: **Difficulty:** ✶✶

- ✓ 500 g salted cod
- ✓ 2 cups milk
- ✓ 2 eggs
- ✓ Olive oil
- ✓ 1 teaspoonful sugar
- ✓ ¼ cup flour

Soak cod in water for 48 hours, changing water every 8 hours. Remove skin and bones, cut into small pieces and place in saucepan; cover with milk and add teaspoonful sugar. Heat, removing from heat when it begins to boil. Remove cod and drain well.
Dip cod in flour and then in beaten egg.
Heat plenty of oil in a frying pan and fry cod until golden on both sides. Serve immediately (though some prefer this dish cold).

Recommended drink: D.O. Valdepeñas Crianza red wine.

SALPICÓN DE MARISCOS
(SEAFOOD COCKTAIL)

Ingredients for 6 people:

Difficulty: ✳

- ✓ 250 g monkfish
- ✓ 250 g langostino prawns
- ✓ 3 tomatoes
- ✓ 1 green pepper
- ✓ ½ small onion
- ✓ 2 tablespoonful sherry vinegar
- ✓ 6 tablespoonful olive oil
- ✓ Salt

Wash monkfish and dry with kitchen roll. Simmer prawns and monkfish in boiling water with salt for 1 minute. Remove and drain.

Wash, dry and chop tomatoes. Chop green pepper. Peel and finely chop onion. Place tomato, pepper and onion in a salad bowl. Add prawns and monkfish and dress with oil, vinegar and salt, mixing well.

Leave to cool for around 2 hours and serve cold.

Recommended drink: Vino D.O. Jerez fino sherry wine.

Ensaladilla de gambas
(Prawn salad)

Ingredients for 8 people: **Difficulty:** ✳✳

✓ 500 g potatoes   ✓ 2 cups mayonnaise

✓ 300 g prawns   ✓ Salt

Peel prawns, put by and place the shells and heads in a pan, covered with water and 1 tablespoonful salt. Simmer for 20 minutes. Wash, peel and dice potatoes. Strain prawn shell stock and boil potatoes in this liquid until cooked. Add prawns and cook for 10 seconds. Strain potatoes and prawns and leave to cool. Mix gently with mayonnaise and allow to cool before serving.

Recommended drink: D.O. Jerez fino sherry wine.

Tartaletas de gulas
(Eel tartlets)

Ingredients for 6 people:

Difficulty: ✳

- ✓ 18 small tartlets
- ✓ 250 g eel
- ✓ 1 clove garlic
- ✓ 6 small tomatoes
- ✓ 1 tablespoonful chopped parsley
- ✓ ½ lemon
- ✓ 5 tablespoonsful virgin olive oil
- ✓ Ground pepper
- ✓ 1 teaspoonful mustard
- ✓ Salt

Wash, dry and quarter small tomatoes, dry and quarter. Wash lemon, dry and grate peel. Squeeze and put juice into a bowl with the lemon peel, the oil, the mustard, salt and pepper. Peel and crush garlic in the mortar or a garlic press and add this to the vinaigrette sauce, stirring well.

Mix the eels with the chopped parsley, tomato and vinaigrette, stirring gently. Stuff tartlets with eels and serve immediately, before they become soft.

Recommended drink: D.O. Txakolí de Vizcaya young white wine.

TAQUITOS DE MERLUZA REBOZADA
(BATTER FRIED HAKE TACOS)

Ingredients for 4 people: **Difficulty:** ✳✳

- ✓ 250 g hake fillets
- ✓ 2 eggs
- ✓ 3 tablespoonsful flour
- ✓ Olive oil
- ✓ Salt

Wash and dry fish, then cut into pieces more or less the same size. Beat eggs in a deep plate with salt.
Heat plenty of oil in a frying pan. Dip fish in flour, then egg, and fry in oil until golden. Remove fish, place on kitchen roll and serve hot.

Recommended drink: D.O. Rías Baixas young white wine.

TOMATITOS RELLENOS DE BACALAO
(SMALL TOMATOES STUFFED WITH COD)

Ingredients for 4 people: **Difficulty:** ✶✶

✓ 200 g salted cod
✓ 8 small tomatoes
✓ 2 cloves garlic

✓ 6 tablespoonsful olive oil
✓ ½ teaspoonful hot paprika

Select firm, ripe tomatoes. Soak cod for 48 hours, changing the water several times. Drain, dry and remove bones. Peel and slice garlic. Heat oil in an earthenware pan with garlic and, when golden, remove from heat. Take out garlic and put by. Add cod to saucepan, stirring with a circular movement to release jelly and cook with the heat it conserves. Remove cod, take off skin and crumble fish into small pieces.

Simmer tomatoes for 6-8 minutes in boiling water, peel, cut off top, carefully empty and fill with cod. Decorate with garlic and paprika and serve immediately.

Recommended drink: D.O. Rueda Crianza white wine.

TOSTADITAS GRATINADAS DE BRANDADA
(BRANDADE GRATINATED TOAST)

Ingredients for 4 people: **Difficulty:** ✳✳

- ✓ 8 slices white bread
- ✓ 200 g crumbled cod
- ✓ ½ cup olive oil
- ✓ ¼ cup milk

- ✓ 1 clove garlic
- ✓ 1 teaspoonful chopped parsley
- ✓ Sesame

Soak crumbled cod in water de 4 a 6 hours to remove salt, changing water from time to time. Drain, place in pan and cover with fresh water. Heat and, before it begins to boil, remove from heat and drain well. In a blender, mix cod with chopped garlic and parsley. Gradually add warm milk and oil, beating all the time until it binds, as if this were a mayonnaise sauce.
Toast bread and spread cream over toast, optionally sprinkling with sesame seeds. Gratinate in hot oven for a few minutes and serve immediately.

Recommended drink: D.O. Tarragona Crianza white wine.

VIEIRAS A LA GALLEGA
(GALICIAN-STYLE SCALLOPS)

Ingredients for 6 people: **Difficulty:** ✸✸

✓ 6 scallops   ✓ 2 tablespoonsful fried tomato   ✓ 5 tablespoonsful olive oil
✓ 1 large onion   ✓ 1 tablespoonful chopped parsley ✓ Ground pepper
✓ 1 clove garlic   ✓ 2 tablespoonsful breadcrumbs   ✓ Salt
✓ ½ cup white wine   ✓ 1 tablespoonful sweet paprika

Wash scallops in cold water, clean with a scrubbing brush and boil in water until they open. Then remove the blackish band around the open scallops and wash them to remove any sand. Peel and chop onion and garlic.

Next, lightly fry onion and garlic in a frying pan with oil. Add paprika, stir and add wine, then reducing a little. Add fried tomato and season with salt and pepper.

Arrange scallops in shells, cover with the sauce and sprinkle with breadcrumbs and parsley. Pour a little oil over the scallops and gratinate in oven. Serve hot.

Recommended drink: D.O. Albariño young white wine.

ANGULAS AL AJILLO
(EELS IN GARLIC)

Ingredients for 4 people:

Difficulty: ✷

- ✓ 250 g eels
- ✓ 2 cloves garlic
- ✓ 4 tablespoonsful olive oil
- ✓ 1 chilli pepper
- ✓ Salt

Pour half oil into each of two earthenware dishes and heat. Add garlic, peeled and sliced, and chilli pepper, chopped. When garlic is golden, add eels, stir with a wooden spoon and remove quickly from heat. Cover and leave for a minute to complete cooking. Add a little salt and serve immediately.

Recommended drink: D.O. Navarra Crianza white wine.

BROCHETAS DE SEPIA
(SQUID BROCHETTES)

Ingredients for 4 people: **Difficulty:** ✳ ✳

- ✓ 16 small squid
- ✓ 2 tablespoonsful olive oil
- ✓ 4 cloves garlic
- ✓ 2 tablespoonsful fried tomato

- ✓ 1 tablespoonful chopped parsley
- ✓ Ground black pepper
- ✓ Salt

Prepare a spicy adobo sauce from the garlic, finely chopped, tomato, parsley, oil, salt and pepper.
Wash the squid and thread onto brochettes. Place brochettes in a dish and spread with the sauce made previously. Leave to rest for one or two hours.
Heat grill or a wide frying pan and fry brochettes until cooked on both sides. Serve hot.

Recommended drink: D.O. Jerez fino sherry wine.

Cocochas en salsa verde
(Cod cheeks in green sauce)

Ingredients for 6 people:

Difficulty: ✹✹

- ✓ 500 g cod cheeks (cod)
- ✓ 1 small onion
- ✓ 2 cloves garlic
- ✓ 2 tablespoonsful chopped parsley
- ✓ ¼ chilli pepper (optional)
- ✓ 3 tablespoonsful virgin olive oil
- ✓ Salt

Wash the cod cheeks and lightly season. Heat oil in an earthenware dish and lightly fry the onion, finally chopped, until transparent; add garlic, sliced, and chilli pepper. When mixture begins to turn golden, add cod cheeks, parsley and salt and stir well with a wooden spoon. Leave on heat until oil starts to boil and the fish starts to separate. Stir saucepan steadily in circular manner until cod cheeks release jelly and oil binds, forming a thick sauce. Serve immediately.

Recommended drink: D.O. Txakolí de Vizcaya white wine.

Tostas de anchoa
(Anchovies on toast)

Ingredients for 6 people:

Difficulty: ✳

- ✓ 12 anchovies in brine
- ✓ 2 tomatoes
- ✓ 1 tablespoonful chopped parsley
- ✓ 6 slices bread
- ✓ 1 little virgin olive oil

Wash the anchovies, separating the fillets and removing skin. Wash in cold water and drain. Arrange on a plate and cover with olive oil; leave for 24 hours.
Toast bread and arrange tomatoes, finely slice, and anchovies on top. Add a little oil and chopped parsley.

Recommended drink: D.O. Yecla young white wine.

CIGALAS A LA PARRILLA
(GRILLED LOBSTER)

Ingredients for 4 people: **Difficulty:** ✷

✓ 800 g Norway lobster   ✓ 1 tablespoonful virgin olive oil

✓ 1 lemon   ✓ Maldon salt (or rock salt)

Wash the lobsters and cut in half, lengthways. Heat grill, pour on a little oil, sprinkle with salt and arrange lobsters on it, meat side up. Grill lobsters until meat loses transparency whilst still retaining juice.
Serve immediately, sprinkling salt and any juice they have given off, accompanied by slices of lemon.

Recommended drink: D.O. Alella young white wine.

BARQUITAS VARIADAS
(BARQUETTES VARIÉES)

Ingredients for 6 people: **Difficulty:** ✳✳

- ✓ 10 small tomatoes
- ✓ 2 cucumbers
- ✓ 2 endives
- ✓ 150 g fresh cheese
- ✓ 1 tablespoonful milk
- ✓ 1 tablespoonful butter

- ✓ Oregano
- ✓ Parsley
- ✓ Fennel
- ✓ 4 black olives
- ✓ 200 g langostino prawns
- ✓ 3 tablespoonsful mayonnaise

- ✓ 1 spring onion
- ✓ 200 g tuna in oil
- ✓ 6 tablespoonsful cream
- ✓ 30 g trout eggs
- ✓ Ground pepper
- ✓ Salt

Scoop out the tomato halves. Mix cheese with milk and butter; add oregano, parsley and fennel. Stuff and adorn with olives.

Peel cucumbers, leaving the skin to one side, cut into thick slices and remove centre, leaving a small base. Chop pulp and mix with prawns, cooked and peeled (putting several by for later), mayonnaise, spring onion, chopped, salt and pepper. Stuff with this mixture and decorate with the prawns you put by earlier.

Remove the outside leaves from the endives, wash and dry. Beat cream and tuna together. Stuff endive leaves with this mixture and decorate with trout eggs.

Recommended drink: D.O. Vino Espumoso Brut Cava.

EMPANADA DE SARDINAS
(BREADED SARDINES)

Ingredients for 12 people:

Difficulty: ✳✳✳

- ✓ 1 kg flour
- ✓ 1 cup olive oil
- ✓ 15 g baking yeast
- ✓ 2 teaspoonsful sweet paprika
- ✓ 2 large onions, peeled and sliced
- ✓ 300 g green peppers, chopped
- ✓ ½ kg sardines
- ✓ 3 cloves garlic
- ✓ Salt

To prepare the filling. Heat half cup oil in a frying pan and lightly fry onion and garlic, peeled and chopped, for 10 minutes. Add peppers and gently fry for another 10 minutes. Add paprika and salt, stir, remove from heat and leave to cool. Drain oil from this filling and put by. Clean and open sardines, removing backbone.

To prepare the dough. Put 6 tablespoonsful oil in a bowl with the yeast, dissolved in warm, salty water. Stir and add flour little by little, kneading to obtain a smooth dough. Cover and leave in bowl for an hour or until it rises. Divide dough into two parts, roll out flat and use one piece to line an oven plate. Spread the filling over the dough and then arrange the sardines, cleaned and boned, on top, neatly aligned. Cover with the other piece of dough and close, pinching edges together. Prick top with a fork and grease with a little oil or beaten egg. Bake in oven at 180° for around 40 minutes until the pastry is crisp.

Recommended drink: D.O. Ribeiro young white wine.

Sepias con ajo y perejil
(Squid with garlic and parsley)

Ingredients for 6 people:

- ✓ 600 g squid
- ✓ 4 cloves garlic
- ✓ 6 tablespoonsful olive oil
- ✓ Parsley
- ✓ Salt

Difficulty: ✶

Clean squid well, removing all insides. Wash inside and outside and dry on kitchen roll. Then heat oil in a frying pan and add garlic, peeled and chopped, squid and parsley. Fry for 4 or 5 minutes, turning once. Season and serve immediately.

Recommended drink: D.O. Alicante Crianza white wine.

HUEVAS ALIÑADAS
(FISH ROE, DRESSED IN A SALAD)

Ingredients for 4 people: **Difficulty:** ✳

✓ 250 g fish roe

✓ 3 tomatoes

✓ 1 green pepper

✓ 1 medium-sized onion

✓ 1 bay leaf

✓ 6 tablespoonsful virgin olive oil

✓ 1 ½ tablespoonful vinegar

✓ Salt

Wash the roe. In a saucepan, heat water, bay leaf, ¼ de onion and salt. Simmer for 10 minutes, add roe and simmer for about 5 minutes. Leave to cool in stock.
Whilst the roe is frying, wash and finely chop tomatoes, pepper and remaining onion. Remove and drain roe and cut into thick slices. Arrange in a serving dish. Dress the tomato, pepper and onion salad with oil, vinegar and salt, and spread over the roe. Leave for a while to allow the roe to absorb this dressing.

Recommended drink: D.O. Jerez fino sherry wine.

EGGS

HUEVOS ESTRELLADOS CON CHORIZO
(FRIED EGGS WITH CHORIZO)

Ingredients for 6 people: **Difficulty:** ✷✷

✓ 500 g potatoes   ✓ 200 g chorizo   ✓ 2 tablespoonsful olive oil

✓ 3 eggs   ✓ ½ cup oil   ✓ Salt

Peel potatoes, wash, and slice into small squares. Simmer in boiling salted water for 10 minutes, remove and drain well.
Heat oil in a frying pan and fry potatoes until lightly golden; remove, drain and put by. Cut chorizo into slices and fry.
Beat eggs as if for an omelette, season and mix with potatoes and chorizo. Heat olive oil in a frying pan and cook eggs, stirring gently. Serve hot.

Recommended drink: D.O. Navarra Crianza red wine.

CANASTILLAS DE HUEVOS
(EGG BASKETS)

Ingredients for 6 people:		Difficulty: ✳✳
✓ 150 g flour	✓ 1 egg yolk	✓ 100 g bacon
✓ 75 g butter	✓ 1 pinch salt	✓ 12 quail's eggs

To prepare the tartlets. Pour flour onto the worktop and form a volcano. Into the "crater", place the butter, in small pieces, the egg yolk, a tablespoonful of cold water and salt. Knead mixture to obtain a smooth dough. Form a ball and leave to rest in fridge for 30 minutes.

Next, roll out the dough into a thin layer and line tartlet moulds. Prick the bottom and sides with a fork and bake in the oven at medium temperature for 10-15 minutes. Remove from oven, allow to cool a little, remove carefully from moulds and allow to cool completely.

To prepare filling. Arrange a layer of bacon, chopped at the bottom of the tartlets. Break a quail's egg into each and cover with more bacon. Place in oven and bake for 3-5 minutes or until the eggs are cooked, but before the yolk becomes hard.

Recommended drink: D.O. Rioja young red wine.

HUEVOS AL CAPOTE
(EGG ON "CLOAK")

Ingredients for 6 people: **Difficulty:** ✶

✓ 12 quail's eggs   ✓ 2 tablespoonsful olive oil

✓ 125 g Iberian ham   ✓ Salt

✓ 12 slices white bread

With a pasta cutter, cut out the centre of the bread slices. Fry in plenty of hot oil and drain on kitchen roll, or toast in oven at low temperature (90°) until golden.
Grease grill or frying pan with oil and fry eggs and ham, chopped. Arrange ham over fried bread, cover with egg, season and serve hot.

Recommended drink: D.O. La Mancha red wine.

MIGAS CON HUEVOS DE CODORNIZ
(BREADCRUMBS WITH QUAIL'S EGGS)

Ingredients for 6 people: **Difficulty: ✳✳**

- ✓ 100 g chorizo
- ✓ 100 g streaky bacon
- ✓ 6 cloves garlic
- ✓ 1 cup water
- ✓ 6 quail's eggs
- ✓ 4 tablespoonsful olive oil
- ✓ 300 g white bread
- ✓ Salt

Slice the bread (preferably from the day before) and place in a bowl. Dissolve salt in water and sprinkle over bread, which should become wet, but not break up. Cover with a cloth and leave for 8-10 hours. Cover the bottom of a frying pan with oil and place over heat. Add whole garlic and fry until golden, then add chorizo and bacon, sliced and diced respectively. When these give off a little fat, add pan, stirring all the time until the crumbs become loose (around 30 minutes).

Finally, in a separate frying pan, fry quail's eggs and serve with the migas on small plates.

Recommended drink: D.O. La Mancha Reserva red wine.

REPÁPALOS
(CROQUETTES)

Ingredients for 10 people:

Difficulty: ✱✱✱

- ✓ 6 eggs
- ✓ 300 g bread
- ✓ 2 sprigs parsley
- ✓ 8 cloves garlic
- ✓ 5 tablespoonsful olive oil
- ✓ 1 medium-sized onion
- ✓ 1 bay leaf
- ✓ 1 cup beef stock
- ✓ Salt

Beat eggs as if for an omelette. Stir in crumbs from bread and knead into dough. In a mortar, grind 6 cloves garlic, 1 sprig of parsley and salt and add to the dough. Mix well, and when bread is spongy, make the repápalos (a kind of small croquette) and fry in plenty of hot oil. Remove, drain and put by.

To make the sauce, chop onion very fine and fry with remaining garlic in a little oil from the repápalos until transparent. Add bay leaf, parsley and stock, and simmer for 5 minutes.

Add the repápalos, not quite covering them with the stock. Simmer for another 5 minutes to absorb flavour. Serve.

Recommended drink: D.O. Costers del Segre Crianza white wine.

REVUELTO DE ERIZOS DE MAR
(SEA URCHIN SCRAMBLED EGGS)

Ingredients for 4 people: **Difficulty:** ✳

✓ 50 g sea urchin eggs   ✓ 2 tablespoonsful olive oil

✓ 2 eggs   ✓ Salt

✓ Ground white pepper

Beat eggs in a bowl with salt and pepper. Use a fork to mash sea urchin eggs, add to eggs and stir well.

Heat oil in a non-stick frying pan and cook the eggs, stirring with a wooden spoon, leaving them soft and juicy. Serve immediately in small dishes or tartlets. Optionally, serve with fried bread.

Recommended drink: D.O. Penedés young white wine.

Huevos rellenos de sardinas
(Sardine stuffed eggs)

Ingredients for 4 people:		Difficulty: ✷✷
✓ 4 eggs	✓ 12 stoned olives	✓ Ground white pepper
✓ 1 tin sardines in oil	✓ 1 tablespoonful chopped parsley	✓ Salt
✓ ½ cup mayonnaise	✓ 1 morrón pepper	

Boil eggs, peel and cut in two, lengthways. Scoop out yolk and place in a separate bowl. Remove bones from sardines.

Use a fork to mash egg yolk. Add sardines, reserving a few pieces for decoration. Stir well, add mayonnaise and mash everything together with a fork to form a paste.

Season with a little pepper and salt to taste. Sprinkle with parsley and stir again.

Pour mixture into a cake decorating bag with wide, serrated nozzle and fill egg whites. Put a little moron pepper into each olive and decorate the eggs with olives and the sardine pieces put by earlier.

Recommended drink: D.O. Cigales rosé wine.

EL PRIVILEGIO DEL CURA
("THE PREACHER'S PRIVILEGE")

Ingredients for 4 people: **Difficulty:** ✳✳✳

- ✓ 4 quail's eggs
- ✓ 150 g minced pork
- ✓ 4 pasta wafers for small pasties
- ✓ 1 cup fried tomato
- ✓ 1 clove garlic
- ✓ ½ cup olive oil
- ✓ Ground pepper
- ✓ 1 teaspoonful oregano
- ✓ 1 bay leaf
- ✓ Salt

Peel and finely chop garlic. Heat 2 tablespoonsful oil in a frying pan and fry garlic until golden. Add minced meat and fry quickly until it breaks up. Season, add fried tomato, half the oregano and the bay leaf. Simmer for 5 minutes and remove from heat.

Heat plenty of oil in a frying pan and fry pastry wafers until crisp and golden. Remove, drain and arrange on 4 side plates. Cover with the meat sauce. Fry eggs and place one on each tartlet. Sprinkle with the rest of the oregano and serve immediately.

Recommended drink: D.O. Cariñena Crianza red wine.

Tortilla de patatas
(Potato omelette)

Ingredients for 6 people: **Difficulty:** ✳✳

✓ 500 g potatoes   ✓ 6 eggs   ✓ Salt

✓ 1 medium-sized onion   ✓ Olive oil for frying

Peel potatoes, wash and cut into thin slices. Season with salt. Finely chop onion.
Fry potatoes with onion on a low heat until tender, without becoming golden. Drain off all oil.
Beat eggs in a bowl, add potatoes with onion and stir well. Pour mixture into frying pan, greased with 2 tablespoonsful hot oil.
Simmer until the omelette cooks well on this side. Raise edges slightly with a spatula to prevent sticking. Use a plate to turn omelette. Heat frying pan and slide omelette from plate back into frying pan to cook the other side. Serve hot or cold.

Recommended drink: D.O. Valdepeñas Crianza red wine.

Tortilla de habas con jamón
(Kidney bean and ham omelette)

Ingredients for 6 people:

Difficulty: ✳✳

- ✓ 6 eggs
- ✓ 50 g serrano cured ham, diced
- ✓ 150 g broad beans, peeled
- ✓ Olive oil for frying
- ✓ Salt

Gently fry the beans in a deep frying pan, covered, with 2 tablespoonsful oil and a little salt. When beans are tender, add ham and stir with a wooden spoon. Put by on kitchen roll. Beat eggs in a bowl, add beans and ham, drained, and cook omelette in a frying pan with one tablespoonful of hot oil. Once cooked on one side, use a plate or saucepan lid to turn it over and cook the other. Serve hot or cold.

Recommended drink: D.O. Yecla young red wine.

Tortilla de ibéricos
(Iberian cold cut omelette)

Ingredients for 8 people:

- 8 eggs
- 200 g potatoes
- 1 large onion
- 75 g serrano cured ham

- 50 g chorizo ibérico
- ½ cup olive oil for frying
- Salt

Difficulty: ✳

Cut potatoes and onion into thin slices and fry in a frying pan with oil, which should not be too hot. Drain. Cut cold meat into small pieces, saving some for decoration, and mix with eggs in a bowl. Add potatoes and onion, season and stir well.
Cook omelette in frying pan with 2 tablespoonsful oil at medium heat, decorate with ham triangles and slices of chorizo, and serve.

Recommended drink: D.O. Bierzo Crianza red wine.

TORTILLA RELLENA DE MORCILLA
(OMELETTE STUFFED WITH MORCILLA)

Ingredients for 8 people: **Difficulty:** ✷✷

✓ 8 eggs   ✓ 1 large onion   ✓ ¾ cups olive oil

✓ 300 g morcilla   ✓ 500 g potatoes   ✓ Salt

On a low heat, gently fry the chopped onion and potatoes, cut into thin slices, in oil until soft. Remove and drain. Whilst potatoes are frying, use scissors to open morcilla skin and remove meat; place in a non-stick frying pan and fry for about 5 minutes, until loose. Divide potato and onion mixture into 4 parts. Beat eggs in bowls in twos, with salt, and mix with one part potato and onion mixture. Cook four thin omelettes serve in twos, filled with the morcilla. Cut omelettes into quarters and accompany with slices of tomato or to taste.

Recommended drink: D.O. Rioja Crianza red wine.

TORTILLA EN SALSA
(OMELETTE IN SAUCE)

Ingredients for 8 people: **Difficulty:** ✳✳✳

- ✓ 250 g potatoes
- ✓ ½ large onion
- ✓ 7 eggs
- ✓ 6 tablespoonsful olive oil
- ✓ 1 tablespoonful flour
- ✓ 1 cup stock
- ✓ 1 clove garlic
- ✓ 1 tablespoonful chopped parsley
- ✓ 2 tablespoonsful white wine
- ✓ Ground pepper
- ✓ Salt

Heat oil in a frying pan and fry potatoes, peeled and thinly sliced, with ½ onion, finely chopped. When soft, but not yet golden, remove, drain and mix with eggs, beaten. Season and cook an omelette in a frying pan. Leave to cool.

Heat oil in a saucepan and lightly fry remaining onion; when golden, add flour, stir and add stock, wine, finely chopped garlic and parsley, salt and pepper and simmer for a few minutes.

Add omelette to the pan and simmer for around 10 minutes approximately. Slice and serve.

Recommended drink: D.O. Navarra Crianza red wine.

TORTILLA MARINERA
(SEAFOOD OMELETTE)

Ingredients for 8 people: **Difficulty:** ✳✳

- ✓ 8 eggs
- ✓ 250 g crab sticks
- ✓ ½ lettuce
- ✓ 1 spring onion
- ✓ 1 onion
- ✓ 250 g potatoes
- ✓ 1 cup mayonnaise
- ✓ ½ yoghurt
- ✓ ½ cup olive oil

Peel potatoes, wash and cut into thin slices. Peel onion and cut into thin slices, or chop. Heat plenty of oil in a frying pan and lightly fry onion until transparent. Add potatoes and fry gently for around 30 minutes or until tender. Remove and drain well.
While potatoes are frying, make a salad with lettuce, spring onion and chopped crab sticks chopped, leaving a few for decoration. Mix yoghurt into mayonnaise to dress salad. Divide potato and onion mixture into 4 parts. Beat eggs in twos and mix with one part potato. Cook four thick, flat omelettes, allow to cool in twos, filled with the salad and decorated with the crab sticks put by.

Recommended drink: D.O. Navarra rosé wine.

MEAT

LIMOSNERAS DE HABITAS Y BUTIFARRA
(BABY BROAD BEAN AND BUTIFARRA SAUSAGE AUMONIERES)

Ingredients for 8 people: **Difficulty:** ✱✱

- ✓ 8 sheets pasta
- ✓ 250 g fresh butifarra sausage
- ✓ 250 g broad beans, loose
- ✓ ½ cup oloroso wine
- ✓ 1 tablespoonful olive oil
- ✓ Ground black pepper
- ✓ 16 sprigs chives
- ✓ Salt

Using scissors, cut skin from sausages and remove meat. Heat oil in a frying pan and fry meat, separating with a fork. When golden, add beans, optionally with their skin removed, and fry for 10 minutes. Drain off excess fat. Sprinkle with wine, season and reduce liquid by half.

Cut pasta sheets in half and spread the above sauce in the centre of each piece, folding the edges over to form little bags. Ties these packages with a long chive or strip from a leek and arrange on an oven tray. Grease with oil and bake in oven for about 8-10 minutes until golden. Serve immediately.

Recommended drink: D.O. Priorat Crianza red wine.

ALBÓNDIGAS EN SALSA PICANTE
(MEAT BALLS IN SPICY SAUCE)

Ingredients for 8 people: **Difficulty:** ✻✻

- ✓ 200 g minced pork
- ✓ 200 g minced beef
- ✓ 1 slice bread, soaked in milk
- ✓ 1 egg
- ✓ 1 teaspoonful concentrated tomato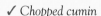
- ✓ Chopped coriander

- ✓ Chopped cumin
- ✓ Salt

For the sauce : 1 cup fresh tomato purée,
1 spring onion, chopped, ½ chilli pepper,
1 clove garlic, chopped, chives, chopped,
1 teaspoonful sugar, 2 tablespoonsful olive oil.

To prepare meat balls. Beat egg in a bowl and mix all ingredients listed to make meat balls. Stir well and form rather small meat balls. Place in a metal baking tray and sprinkle with oil. Heat oven and bake meat balls at 200° for 10-15 minutes.

To prepare the sauce. Heat oil in a frying pan and fry spring onion, garlic and chilli pepper. After 5 minutes, add other ingredients and lightly fry for 10-15 minutes. Serve meat balls hot on a plate or dish, accompanied by sauce in a bowl.

Recommended drink: D.O. Ribera del Duero Crianza red wine.

Terrina de conejo
(Terrine of rabbit)

Ingredients for 8 people:

Difficulty: ✻✻✻

- ✓ 1 ¼ kg rabbit
- ✓ 250 g minced pork
- ✓ 100 g minced beef
- ✓ 200 g streaky bacon
- ✓ 1 medium-sized onion
- ✓ 1 carrot and 1 leek
- ✓ 1 sprig celery
- ✓ 2 eggs
- ✓ ½ cup cream
- ✓ 2 tablespoonsful olive oil
- ✓ 1 sprig aromatic herbs
- ✓ 6 grains pepper and salt

Remove meat from rabbit bones, put by meat and fry bones until golden in a pan with oil, onion, carrots, celery and leek, washed and chopped; and sprig aromatic herbs and grain pepper and cover with water; simmer for 1 hour. Drain stock and simmer in a pan, scooping froth from surface, reducing it to a thick liquid.

Chop rabbit meat and mix with pork and beef, eggs, cream, salt, ground pepper and the stock prepared earlier. Line a mould with bacon slices, allowing the ends to overflow the mould. Pour in mixture and fold bacon slices back over filling. Cover mould with silver paper and bake in bain marie in oven at medium temperature media for one hour or until cooked. Remove from oven and place a weight on top until the dish cools. Serve with toast.

Recommended drink: D.O. Binissalem Crianza red wine.

ALITAS ADOBADAS
(SPICY CHICKEN WINGS)

Ingredients for 8 people: **Difficulty:** ✳✳

- ✓ 1 kg chicken wings
- ✓ 4 tablespoonsful light honey
- ✓ 2 tablespoonsful apricot jam
- ✓ 1 tablespoonful ground ginger

- ✓ 2 cloves garlic, crushed
- ✓ 1 tablespoonful soya sauce
- ✓ 1 tablespoonful ketchup
- ✓ Salt

Wash wings and dry with kitchen roll. Place remaining ingredients in a pan and heat gently for 5 minutes.

Place the wings in a recipient, pour on the marinade, cover recipient and leave to rest for 2 hours.

Remove wings from marinade and grill on the barbeque for around 15-20 minutes or until cooked and golden. Serve with sauces to taste.

Recommended drink: D.O. Jerez Oloroso Seco sherry wine.

BANDERILLAS EN BECHAMEL
(CHICKEN BROCHETTES IN BÉCHAMEL SAUCE)

Ingredients for 4 people: **Difficulty:** ✳✳✳

✓ 200 g chicken breast, cooked   ✓ 1 egg

✓ 1 cup béchamel sauce   ✓ ¼ cup olive oil

✓ 1 tablespoonful breadcrumbs   ✓ Salt

Dice chicken breast. Thread three pieces of chicken each onto wooden or metal skewers and season. Dip in béchamel until covered and leave to cool on marble or other flat surface.
Beat egg in a deep plate and dip brochettes, firstly in the egg and then in breadcrumbs. Fry in plenty of hot oil. Drain on kitchen roll and serve hot.

Recommended drink: D.O. Valdepeñas Crianza red wine.

BOLITAS DE CODORNIZ
(QUAIL BALLS)

Ingredients for 6 people: **Difficulty:** ✳✳

- ✓ 12 quail drumsticks
- ✓ 2 cloves garlic
- ✓ 2 tablespoonsful white wine
- ✓ 2 bay leaves
- ✓ 2 tablespoonsful ketchup
- ✓ 1 teaspoonful olive oil
- ✓ ¼ cup soya sauce
- ✓ Salt

Clean quail legs, dry and carefully remove upper bone to leave drumsticks. Pull on the meat to drag it to one end to form a ball, so that the bone can be picked up in the fingers. Place quail drumsticks in a bowl or deep dish.

Peel garlic, chop in mortar and mix with wine, chopped bay leaf, ketchup, salt and oil. Spread evenly over drumsticks. Leave to soak for at least 30 minutes (they can even be left overnight).

Place drumsticks in a metal tray and bake in oven, preheated to 180° C, for around 30 minutes, until golden. Serve hot, accompanied by the soya sauce in a separate bowl.

Recommended drink: D.O. Valdepeñas Crianza red wine.

PINCHOS DE MELÓN CON JAMÓN
(MELON AND HAM BROCHETTES)

Ingredients for 4 people: **Difficulty:** ✳

- ✓ 400 g melon
- ✓ 150 g Iberian ham
- ✓ 150 g prawns
- ✓ 1 pinch paprika

- ✓ 3 tablespoonsful virgin olive oil
- ✓ 1 tablespoonful sherry vinegar
- ✓ Chive
- ✓ Salt

Cut melon into balls or cubes, all more or less the same size, and place in a bowl. In a cup, mix oil, vinegar, salt and paprika. Pour over melon, stir and leave for around 10 minutes. Cut ham into small slices and thread them onto skewers, alternating with melon pieces. Thread brochettes on pieces of melon peel or similar. Fry peeled prawns on grill or in hot frying pan hot and thread on onto the end of each brochette. Sprinkle with chives and serve.

Recommended drink: D.O. Vino Espumoso Brut Cava.

PINCHITOS DE POLLO
(SMALL CHICKEN BROCHETTES)

Ingredients for 4 people: **Difficulty:** ✳✳

- ✓ 250 g chicken breast
- ✓ ½ cup white wine
- ✓ ½ cup water
- ✓ 2 tablespoonful olive oil
- ✓ 1 tablespoonful sweet paprika

- ✓ ½ tablespoonful hot paprika
- ✓ Oregano
- ✓ 1 bay leaf
- ✓ 2 cloves garlic
- ✓ Salt

Wash chicken breast and dry with kitchen roll. Slice chicken into long pieces and place in a bowl. Season and add garlic, peeled and crushed, wine, water, oil, both the hot and the sweet paprika, oregano and bay leaf. Stir well and leave in this marinade for at least 2 hours.

Next, thread the chicken pieces onto cocktail sticks and grill with 2 tablespoonsful oil. Serve hot.

Recommended drink: D.O. Ribera del Duero young red wine.

CHULETITAS DE CONEJO
(SMALL RABBIT RIBS)

Ingredients for 4 people: **Difficulty:** ✳

- ✓ 200 g rabbit ribs
- ✓ 1 tablespoonful vinegar
- ✓ 1 tablespoonful brown sugar
- ✓ 1 tablespoonful cornflour
- ✓ ½ cup chicken stock

- ✓ 1 sprig thyme
- ✓ 3 tablespoonsful oil
- ✓ Ground pepper
- ✓ Salt

Season rabbit ribs and fry in hot oil until golden (make sure they are not overcooked). Put by, keeping warm.

To the fat from frying the ribs, add sugar, vinegar, thyme, salt, pepper and cornflour, dissolved in stock. Simmer, stirring with a wooden spoon, until the sauce binds. Serve rabbit ribs immediately, spread with the sauce.

Recommended drink: D.O. Binissalem Crianza red wine.

Costillas marinadas al comino
(Chops marinated in cumin)

Ingredients for 8 people:

Difficulty: ✳✳

- ✓ 500 g pork chops
- ✓ 4 cloves garlic
- ✓ 1 tablespoonful cumin
- ✓ 1 tablespoonful sherry vinegar
- ✓ 2 tablespoonsful olive oil
- ✓ 2 tablespoonsful fried tomato
- ✓ 1 teaspoonful sugar
- ✓ Thyme
- ✓ Ground pepper
- ✓ Salt

Wash chops and place in a deep dish. Peel garlic and crush in mortar with cumin, salt and pepper. Add vinegar, sugar, tomato, thyme, salt and pepper; stir and pour over the chops, spreading it all over. Cover with kitchen films and leave to marinate for a couple of hours.

Place chops, with sauce, on a metal oven tray, sprinkle with oil and bake in a hot oven at 180° for 30 minutes, until crisp and golden. Serve hot.

Recommended drink: D.O. Cariñena Crianza red wine.

CRIADILLAS DE CORDERO EMPANADAS
(BREADED LAMB TESTICLES)

Ingredients for 4 people: **Difficulty:** ✳✳

✓ *8 lamb testicles*   ✓ *2 tablespoonsful breadcrumbs*

✓ *2 eggs*   ✓ *4 tablespoonsful oil*

✓ *Ground pepper*   ✓ *Salt*

Remove skin from testicles and cut into slices 1 cm thick. Place in a recipient, cover with salted water and leave for 1 hour. Drain and dry with kitchen roll.
Beat eggs on a plate and place breadcrumbs on a separate plate. Heat plenty of oil in a frying pan; season the testicles, dip in egg and breadcrumbs, in that order, and fry in hot oil until golden. Drain on kitchen roll and serve with chips or salad.

Recommended drink: D.O. Navarra rosé wine.

Croquetas de ibérico
(Iberian ham croquettes)

Ingredients for 8 people:

Difficulty: ✳✳✳

- ✓ 100 g Iberian ham
- ✓ 2 ½ tablespoonsful flour
- ✓ 1 cup olive oil
- ✓ 2 cups milk
- ✓ 2 eggs
- ✓ 1 teaspoonful butter
- ✓ 40 g breadcrumbs
- ✓ Salt

Cut the ham into very thin slices. Heat 2 tablespoonsful oil and the butter in a saucepan or frying pan and add flour. Stir quickly with a wooden spoon and add milk little by little, stirring all the time. Once you have added half the milk, add ham and continue to stir to form a smooth, even cream. Simmer for around 5 minutes. Add salt to taste. Pour into a dish and leave to cool.

Use two spoons or hands to make croquettes and dip in eggs, beaten, followed by breadcrumbs. Heat plenty of oil in a deep frying pan and fry croquettes until golden. Drain on kitchen roll and serve hot.

Recommended drink: D.O. Ribera del Guadiana Crianza red wine.

Delicias de chistorra
(Chistorra sausage delights)

Ingredients for 8 people: **Difficulty:** ✳✳

✓ 250 g pastry dough   ✓ 200 g chistorra sausage   ✓ 1 egg

Roll out pastry and cut as many slices as you have slices of chistorra, which should be a little more narrow. Roll each chistorra piece in a slice of pastry, gluing the edges with beaten egg. Daub pastry with egg and bake in preheated oven at medium-high temperature until pastry is crisp and golden.
Serve hot from oven.

Recommended drink: D.O. Rioja Crianza red wine.

CHORIZO A LA SIDRA
(CHORIZO SAUSAGE IN CIDER)

Ingredients for 4 people: **Difficulty:** ✱

✓ *250 g chorizo*   ✓ *1 litre cider*

Chop chorizo into slices approximately 3 cm thick.
Place these in an earthenware bowl and cover with cider. Simmer for around 10 minutes and serve, preferably hot.

Recommended drink: Asturian cider.

CALLOS A LA MADRILEÑA
(MADRID STYLE TRIPE)

Ingredients for 12 people: **Difficulty:** ✳✳✳

✓ 1 kg tripe
✓ ½ beef hoof
✓ 100 g serrano cured ham
✓ 300 g chorizo sausage
✓ 300 g morcilla sausage

✓ 1 large onion
✓ 1 tomato
✓ 1 tablespoonful flour
✓ 1 bay leaf
✓ Chilli pepper

✓ 2 cloves garlic
✓ 3 sprigs parsley
✓ Saffron
✓ Salt

Wash tripe and beef well, place in a pan, cover with water with salt and simmer until tender (approximately 2 hours).

Then heat oil in a frying pan and fry chopped onion until golden. Add tomato, skinned and chopped, stir, add flour, simmer and add part of the stock from cooking the tripe.

Next, pour the contents of the frying pan into the saucepan with ham, chorizo, morcilla, bay leaf and chilli pepper (optional), along with chopped garlic, salt, parsley and saffron. Cover and simmer for another 30 minutes, until the stock is good and thick.

Recommended drink: D.O. Madrid Reserva red wine.

Fiambre de pavo al oloroso
(Roast turkey in oloroso wine)

Ingredients for 8 people: **Difficulty:** ✳✳

- ✓ 300 g turkey breast
- ✓ 150 g York ham
- ✓ 1 egg
- ✓ 1 sprig parsley
- ✓ Oregano
- ✓ 1/3 cup oloroso wine
- ✓ 30 g Iberian ham
- ✓ 15 g breadcrumbs
- ✓ Ground pepper and salt

Slice turkey breast and York ham. In a bowl, mix turkey with all other ingredients except Iberian ham.

Take a sheet of silver paper and place over a flat surface. Place half the meat on this, sprinkle the Iberian ham slices over this and, finally, spread the rest of the meat on top. Make a roll by pressing with the hands and wrap in silver paper. Heat oven and bake at medium heat for around 30 minutes. Leave to cool, placing a moderate weight on top, cut into thin slices and serve.

Recommended drink: D.O. Cigales rosé wine.

Brochetas de riñones de cordero
(Lamb kidney brochettes)

Ingredients for 4 people: **Difficulty: ✷✷**

- ✓ 8 lamb kidney
- ✓ 2 cloves garlic
- ✓ 1 tablespoonful vinegar
- ✓ 2 tablespoonsful olive oil

- ✓ 4 bay leaves
- ✓ 8 tomatoes cherry
- ✓ 1 medium-sized onion
- ✓ Thyme

- ✓ Ground black pepper
- ✓ Oregano
- ✓ Ground cumin
- ✓ 1 cup salty water

In a saucepan, mix garlic, peeled and chopped, herbs (except bay leaf), 1 cup water, oil, vinegar, salt and ground pepper. Simmer for 6-7 minutes.

Clean, wash, dry and slice kidneys. Peel and chop onion and cut bay leaves in half. Thread slices of kidney, onion, tomato and bay leaf onto skewers. Spread with sauce and leave to rest for 2-3 hours.

Fry brochettes on the grill or barbeque or in a non-stick frying pan. Serve on a bed of white rice or with salad.

Recommended drink: D.O. La Mancha Crianza red wine.

RIÑONES AL JEREZ
(KIDNEYS IN SHERRY)

Ingredients for 8 people: **Difficulty:** ✷✷

✓ 500 g beef kidneys   ✓ 4 tablespoonsful olive oil

✓ 2 cloves garlic   ✓ 3 tablespoonsful dry sherry

✓ 1 tablespoonful chopped parsley   ✓ Ground black pepper and salt

Clean and wash kidneys well, then slice. Put by.

Heat water in a pan and, once boiling, place kidneys in a colander and the colander in the pan, so that the kidneys cook in steam, not water. Cook in this way for 10 minutes so that kidneys lose all their liquid.

Heat oil in a frying pan and fry garlic until golden. Add kidneys, fry at medium heat, stirring from time to time, until golden. Season and sprinkle with sherry. Add parsley, simmer for a few minutes, remove from heat and serve immediately.

Recommended drink: D.O. Rioja Reserva red wine.

117

SOLOMILLITOS A LA SEVILLANA
(SEVILLE-STYLE PORK FILLETS)

Ingredients for 8 people: **Difficulty: ✶✶**

- ✓ 500 g pork fillets
- ✓ 100 g stoned olives
- ✓ 250 g fresh tomato, chopped
- ✓ 1 onion
- ✓ 2 cloves garlic
- ✓ 1 teaspoonful oregano
- ✓ Ground black pepper
- ✓ 5 tablespoonsful olive oil
- ✓ Salt

Clean fillets and dry with kitchen roll. Slice fairly thickly. Heat oil in a frying pan and quickly fry on both sides. Remove from pan and put by. Peel and chop onion and garlic and gently fry in this oil for around 10 minutes; add tomato and simmer for another 15-20 minutes.

Pour garlic and onion sauce into a pan, season and add fillets, oregano and olives; simmer together for another 10 minutes at lowest heat Serve fillets with chips or to taste.

Recommended drink: D.O. Jerez fino sherry wine.

Solomillo con cebolla confitada
(Iberian pork fillet with onion confit)

Ingredients for 8 people:

Difficulty: ✴✴

- ✓ 400 g fillet Iberian pork
- ✓ 1 onion
- ✓ 10 g Corinth raisins
- ✓ 10 g golden raisins
- ✓ 3 tablespoonsful olive oil
- ✓ 1 tablespoonful sugar
- ✓ Ginger
- ✓ ½ teaspoonful powdered cinnamon
- ✓ Ground pepper
- ✓ Salt

Peel onion and cut into thin slices. Heat 2 tablespoonsful oil in saucepan or deep frying pan and lightly fry onion, gently, until transparent. Add raisins, sugar, cinnamon, ginger and salt. Cover and simmer until onion is golden and slightly caramelised. Remove from heat and put by.

Wash meat and dry with kitchen roll. Season and lightly fry in remaining oil, taking care not to overcook. Arrange onion over fillets and serve.

Recommended drink: D.O. Ribera del Guadiana Reserva red wine.

Tostaditas de sobrasada
(Sobrasada sausage on toast)

Ingredients for 6 people:

Difficulty: ✳

✓ 6 slices white bread   ✓ 150 g sobrasada red sausage   ✓ 3 tablespoonsful sugar

Remove crusts from bread and cut into oval or square shapes, according to taste. Place bread slices in toaster and toast both sides. Spread with a generous layer of sobrasada red sausage and arrange on baking tray.

Sprinkle a little sugar over the middle of the pieces of toast, then grill until sobrasada becomes golden and starts to melt.

Recommended drink: D.O. Pla i Llevant Crianza red wine.

PECHUGAS EN ESCABECHE
(CHICKEN BREASTS IN MARINADE SAUCE)

Ingredients for 12 people: **Difficulty:** ✳✳

✓ 600 g chicken breast   ✓ ½ cup white wine   ✓ The peel from one dried orange
✓ 3 carrots   ✓ ½ cup vinegar   ✓ Thyme
✓ 2 medium-sized onions   ✓ 2 bay leaves   ✓ 8 tablespoonsful olive oil
✓ 3 cloves garlic   ✓ 3 grains black pepper   ✓ Salt

Wash and dry chicken breasts. Heat 8 tablespoonsful oil in a frying pan and fry on either side until golden. Remove and place in a large saucepan.

Place 2 tablespoonsful oil in frying pan and lightly fry bay leaf and thyme, adding this mixture to the pan with the chicken breasts.

Add sliced garlic, onion, sliced into rings, chopped carrots, pepper grains and sale, and lightly fry together for 5 minutes.

Add wine, vinegar and water to cover chicken breasts. Cover and simmer for another 20 minutes. Add the orange peel and leave to cool. Slice chicken and serve in sauce.

Recommended drink: Beer.

POLLO AL AJILLO
(CHICKEN IN GARLIC SAUCE)

Ingredients for 8 people: **Difficulty:** ✳

- ✓ 750 g chicken
- ✓ 10 cloves garlic
- ✓ ¼ cup white wine

- ✓ 6 tablespoonsful olive oil
- ✓ Ground pepper
- ✓ Salt

Cut chicken into fairly small pieces, wash, dry and drain well. Season.
Heat oil in a frying pan and add chicken, stirring often for 5 minutes as it slowly cooks.
Add garlic, peeled and chopped, and continue frying until golden all over. Add wine, stir
and simmer until chicken is also golden and wine evaporates. Serve hot. (This dish is usually eaten with the hands).

Recommended drink: D.O. Valdepeñas Crianza red wine.

TOSTAS DE MORCILLA
(MORCILLA SAUSAGE ON TOAST)

Ingredients for 6 people: *Difficulty:* ✳✳

- ✓ *300 g onion morcilla sausages*
- ✓ *4 eggs*
- ✓ *1 tablespoonful pine seeds*

- ✓ *2 tablespoonsful Corinth raisins*
- ✓ *4 slices white bread*
- ✓ *2 tablespoonsful grated cheese and salt*

Cut skin from morcilla sausages and remove meat, crumbling into small pieces. Place frying pan on heat and add morcilla, stirring with a wooden spoon until becomes cooked and loose. Add raisins and pine seeds, stir to mix well and remove from heat.

Toast bread in oven to prepare at the same time. Beat eggs in a bowl with salt. Add morcilla and stir well. Heat a non-stick frying pan and pour eggs and morcilla into pan. Simmer and stir until cooked, ensuring that the mixture remains juicy.

Spread this mixture over the toast, sprinkle with grated cheese and gratinate under grill for a few seconds. Crackers can also be used instead of toast, for a more crunchy flavour.

Recommended drink: D.O. Somontano Crianza red wine.

MISCELLANY

Plato de ibéricos
(Iberian cold cuts)

Ingredients for 12 people: **Difficulty:** ✳

- ✓ 200 g Iberian bellota ham
- ✓ 200 g Iberian bellota salchichón
- ✓ 200 g Iberian bellota lomo (cured pork loin)
- ✓ 200 g Iberian bellota chorizo
- ✓ 16 slices bread
- ✓ 2 ripe tomatoes
- ✓ Extra virgin olive oil
- ✓ Salt

Cut all the cold meats into thin slices and leave for 10 minutes to reach room temperature. Cut tomatoes in half and spread pulp over bread. Add a few drops of oil and sprinkle a little salt on top. Arrange cold meats attractively on a large plat, accompanied by the tomato bread.

Recommended drink: D.O. Valdepeñas Crianza red wine.

Paella mixta
(Mixed paella)

Ingredients for 10 people:

Difficulty: ✳✳

- ✓ 350 g rice
- ✓ ½ chicken
- ✓ 2 small squid
- ✓ 250 g langostino prawns
- ✓ 500 g cooked mussels
- ✓ ½ red pepper and ½ green pepper
- ✓ 2 ripe tomatoes
- ✓ 5 artichoke hearts
- ✓ 100 g podded peas
- ✓ 2 cloves garlic
- ✓ 6 threads saffron
- ✓ 1/3 teaspoonful sweet paprika
- ✓ 2 cups stock
- ✓ 5 tablespoonsful olive oil
- ✓ Chopped parsley and salt

Heat oil in large, round, shallow pan (paella) and lightly fry chicken, washed and cut up into small pieces, until golden. Add squid, sliced into rings, peppers, sliced, tomatoes, peeled and chopped, peas and artichoke hearts; stir and simmer on a medium heat for 12-15 minutes, stirring with a wooden spoon.

In a mortar, grind garlic, saffron, paprika, parsley and salt, and add to the paella. Add rice and simmer. Mix together the liquid used to open mussels and from cooking langostino prawns with the fish stock (two parts stock for one part rice). Pour hot stock over rice, season and simmer at high heat for 5 minutes. Lower heat and simmer for another 15 minutes. Decorate with mussels and langostino prawns and leave to rest for 4-5 minutes before serving.

Recommended drink: D.O. Utiel-Requena rosé wine.

Bolitas de Cabrales
(Cabrales cheese balls)

Ingredients for 4 people: **Difficulty:** ✳✳

- ✓ 150 g Cabrales cheese
- ✓ 2 tablespoonsful flour
- ✓ 1 cup milk
- ✓ 2 tablespoonsful chopped parsley
- ✓ 40 g butter
- ✓ 2 eggs
- ✓ 3 tablespoonsful breadcrumbs
- ✓ ½ cup oil
- ✓ Salt

Blend cheese and half the milk. Melt butter in frying pan and lightly fry the flour, stirring all the time with a wooden spoon. Immediately, still stirring all the time, gradually add the rest of the milk, little by little, adding a little more milk if necessary. When the sauce begins to thicken, added blended cheese and milk, salt and parsley. Stir and simmer for around 8 minutes. Pour into a dish and leave to cool.

Once the mass is cold, form cheese balls and dip them firstly in the beaten eggs and secondly in the breadcrumbs. Fry in plenty of hot oil. Drain on kitchen roll and serve hot.

Recommended drink: D.O. Somontano Crianza red wine.

CARACOLES EN SALSA
(SNAILS IN SAUCE)

Ingredients for 8 people:

Difficulty: ✳✳

- ✓ ½ kg snails
- ✓ 80 g serrano cured ham
- ✓ 200 g fresh tomato, chopped
- ✓ 2 choricero peppers
- ✓ ½ chilli pepper
- ✓ 1 small onion
- ✓ ½ cup dry white wine
- ✓ 1 bay leaf
- ✓ 5 tablespoonsful olive oil
- ✓ 1 morrón pepper
- ✓ Salt

Clean snails (which should be well purged) well, washing them several times in salted water, then boil them in a pan with plenty of cold water. Add salt, bay leaf and win and summer for between 90 minutes and 2 hours. Scoop off froth. Heat oil in a frying pan and lightly fry the chopped onion, tomato and the pulp from the choricero peppers (previously soaked). Halfway through frying, add ham, diced, then continue frying until all water has evaporated and only oil remains.

Strain snails and put them into the frying pan with the chilli pepper and the morrón pepper, chopped. Cover and simmer for 40 minutes on very low heat.

Recommended drink: D.O. Rueda Crianza white wine.

BOCADITOS DE PLÁTANO
(BANANA FINGER SANDWICHES)

Ingredients for 6 people: **Difficulty:** ✳

✓ 3 bananas   ✓ 200 g bacon

Peel bananas and cut into pieces approximately 4 cm long. Then remove rind from bacon and wrap rashers around banana pieces, securing with a cocktail stick.
Heat oil in a non-stick frying pan and fry the finger sandwiches until the bacon is crisp and golden. Serve hot.

Recommended drink: D.O. Cigales rosé wine.

Torta del Casar con jamón
(Torta del Casar cheese with ham)

Ingredients for 4 people:

Difficulty: ✳

✓ 150 g serrano cured ham   ✓ 150 g Torta del Casar cheese   ✓ 4 slices bread

Lightly toast the bread. Cut the ham and the cheese into slices of more or less the same size as the bread. Place a slice of ham on each piece, with a piece of cheese on top. Bake in oven until the cheese begins to melt. Serve immediately.

Recommended drink: D.O. Rioja Crianza white wine.

EGGS

MEAT

MISCELLANY